THEATRE FOR SHAKESPEARE

THE ALEXANDER LECTURESHIP

THE ALEXANDER LECTURESHIP was founded in honour of Professor W. J. Alexander, who held the Chair of English at University College from 1889 to 1926. Each year the Lectureship brings to the University a distinguished scholar or critic to give a course of lectures on a subject related to English Literature.

THEATRE FOR

SHAKESPEARE

Alfred Harbage

UNIVERSITY OF TORONTO PRESS

TYPOGRAPHY AND DECORATIONS BY ANTJE LINGNER

THE ALEXANDER LECTURES

(Unless otherwise indicated the lectures have been
published by the University of Toronto Press)

1929-30 L. F. CAZAMIAN: Parallelism in the recent development of English and French literature
These lectures were included in the author's *Criticism in
the Making* (Macmillan, 1929)

1930-31 H. W. GARROD: *The Study of Poetry* (Clarendon,
1936)

1931-32 IRVING BABBITT: Wordsworth and modern poetry
Included as "The Primitivism of Wordsworth" in the
author's *On Being Creative* (Houghton, 1932)

1932-33 W. A. CRAIGIE: *The Northern Element in English
Literature* (1933)

1933-34 H. J. C. GRIERSON: Sir Walter Scott
Included in *Sir Walter Scott, Bart.* (Constable, 1938)

1934-35 G. G. SEDGEWICK: *Of Irony, Especially in Drama*
(1934, 1948)

1935-36 E. E. STOLL: *Shakespeare's Young Lovers* (Oxford,
1937)

1936-37 F. B. SNYDER: *Robert Burns, His Personality, His
Reputation, and His Art* (1936)

1937-38 D. NICHOL SMITH: *Some Observations on Eighteenth-
Century Poetry* (1937)

1938-39 CARLETON W. STANLEY: *Matthew Arnold* (1938)

1939-40 J. DOUGLAS N. BUSH: *The Renaissance and English
Humanism* (1939)

1940-41 No lectures given

1941–42　H. J. DAVIS: *Stella, a Gentlewoman of the Eighteenth Century* (Macmillan, 1942)

1942–43　H. GRANVILLE-BARKER: Coriolanus
Included in the author's *Prefaces to Shakespeare: Vol. II* (Princeton, 1947)

1943–44　F. P. WILSON: *Elizabethan and Jacobean* (Clarendon, 1945)

1944–45　F. O. MATTHIESSEN: *Henry James, the Major Phase* (Oxford, 1944)

1945–46　S. C. CHEW: *The Virtues Reconciled, an Iconographical Study* (1947)

1946–47　MARJORIE HOPE NICOLSON: *Voyages to the Moon* (Macmillan, 1948)

1947–48　G. B. HARRISON: Shakespearean Tragedy
Included in the author's *Shakespeare's Tragedies* (Routledge and Kegan Paul, 1951)

1948–49　E. M. W. TILLYARD: *Shakespeare's Problem Plays* (1949)

1949–50　E. K. BROWN: *Rhythm in the Novel* (1950)

1950–51　MALCOLM W. WALLACE: *English Character and the English Literary Tradition* (1952)

1951–52　R. S. CRANE: *The Languages of Criticism and the Structure of Poetry* (1953)

1952–53　No lectures given

1953–54　F. M. SALTER: *Mediaeval Drama in Chester* (1955)

1954–55　ALFRED HARBAGE: *Theatre for Shakespeare* (1955)

1955–56　LEON EDEL: *Literary Biography* (1957)

1956–57　JAMES SUTHERLAND: *On English Prose* (1957)

TO GEORGE F. REYNOLDS

PREFACE

KNOWLEDGE OF THE ELIZABETHAN THEATRE
and its methods is garnered in the hope that modern producers
of Shakespeare will seek to apply it. I was following in the
steps of many distinguished garnerers in this field when I was
honoured with the invitation to give the Alexander Lectures.
I decided to abandon my plan to supply more knowledge, and
to cope instead with the question of its application. If my
lectures prove this decision to have been rash, they may still
serve a useful purpose, in reducing the distress of those who
lament that students emerge too infrequently from their
studies. If any further effect is achieved, it is peculiarly appropriate that the University of Toronto should have given me my
rostrum. The University and the city and province it serves are
displaying a keen interest in Shakespearean production and in
ways it may be improved. I wish to record my gratitude to
my hosts for their cordiality and their tolerance.

My thanks go also to those who had consented to discuss my
subject with me, chiefly persons long concerned with the
application of Elizabethan staging methods: John C. Adams,
Bernard Beckerman, Henry Wells, Angus L. Bowmer, Allar-
dyce Nicoll, Richard Southern, and others. Tyrone Guthrie
and Bernard Miles were generous of their time in London, and
Frederic Halaman and Dimitrios Rondiris in Athens. Even
those who differed most widely from me in point of view
remained patient in spite of my somewhat inquisitorial
approach. My debt to Mr. Rondiris is of a special kind. As

General Director of the National Theatre of Greece, he invited me to attend his rehearsals of *Hippolytus*, and it was while I was observing the selfless devotion of him and his company that I came to realize what a theatre for Shakespeare should be.

A Guggenheim Fellowship for 1953–54 afforded me the chance to compare the methods of several different nations in bringing their ancient masterpieces to the modern stage, as well as to complete my examination of Elizabethan theatrical materials. The latter work was done in the Widener Library, the Folger Library, and the British Museum. My obligation is great to the staffs of these institutions and of the Simon E. Guggenheim Memorial Foundation.

The essay forming Appendix A is reprinted from the *Shakespeare Jahrbuch* of 1955 with the permission of its editors, and that forming Appendix B is abbreviated from an article that appeared originally in the *Publications of the Modern Language Association* of 1933. The latter is of dubious value so far as my present aims are concerned and was included as a personal indulgence. This small book contains all I have said or am likely to say upon its particular subject.

The lectures are printed precisely as they were delivered, and their tone is not always polite. I might plead the sanction of the father who chastises the son in whom he delights. I can more honestly point out Shakespearean production is too tough a perennial to be blighted by an astringent.

A. H.

Harvard University
September, 1955

CONTENTS

I. THE PROBLEM

 TTENDING A PERFORMANCE OF OTHELLO SOME years ago were two ladies whose cheerful and unconscious martyrdom still serves me as a symbol. It became evident as the evening wore on that they were being detained beyond their usual bedtime. The one less successful in controlling the symptoms turned at last to her companion with a whispered apology: "Shakespeare always makes me sleepy, he's so *rhythmic!*"—a delightful utterance, exculpating at once both the poetry-lover and her poet. When the play ended they sidled to the aisle, beaming the contentment of so many good people upon leaving church or a Shakespearean performance, gratified that they have come, and gratified that they now may go.

Perhaps I remember them because I was equally though less graciously bored. Yet the production was one still reckoned as memorable—lavishly mounted, and enriched by the talents of two famous actors. Indeed the audience as a whole was bored, although most of its members would have indignantly denied it and the interval was murmurous with well-bred approval. The word *bored* is scarcely precise: the mood at this as at most performances of Shakespeare might better be described as reverently unreceptive. There was small sense of joy, small sense of sorrow; there was rarely a moment of that hush of absorption which is the only sign-warrant of effectual drama. The average motion picture casts a deeper spell of illusion and wins a stronger emotional response than the tragedies of Shakespeare as staged in our theatres.

A thousand authors have written a thousand critiques of *Othello, Hamlet, Macbeth,* and *Lear,* not always humbly or in a spirit of accord, yet all deferring to the simple judgment that these plays are very beautiful and very sad. They should seem so when performed. The departing spectators should not speak of the accessories of the production as they usually do, sometimes as if from prepared notes, but of the wonder of human destiny as figured forth in the fabled events and the matchless speech of the play itself, or, better still, should preserve an exalted, or at least decent, silence. If these words sound evangelical, if it be objected that aesthetic and emotional response on an appropriately Shakespearean scale would be too fatiguing for modern nerves, let me reduce my demands and ask only that audiences be no less moved by Shakespeare than by lesser dramatists. My grief is that they are rarely moved at all. One observes at performances of *Othello* a disposition to view the proceedings with concern only at the moment when the Moor is smothering the lady, and so might reasonably conclude that the play is defective, that the Moor should have been provided with more ladies to smother and with much earlier occasions. And at *Hamlet, Macbeth,* and even *Lear*— to ascribe these dry eyes about us to a response too deep for tears would be, if I may say so, a little disingenuous.

Now it might seem unlikely, if what I am saying is true, that so many people should attend the performances. Of course a great many others do not. Of my own acquaintance are several who love Shakespeare and love the theatre but do not love Shakespeare in the theatre. One of them tells me that he rarely attends and then always to rediscover that his favourite commentator is Shakespeare's own Christopher Sly— "A very excellent piece of work.... Would 'twere done." If more people are drawn to the theatre by Shakespeare than by any other dramatist, the explanation lies less in the quality of the resulting experience than in the bare statement of the fact: they are drawn to the theatre by *Shakespeare*. His name has come to stand for that whole elusive but ever-beckoning complex of moral and cultural values proverbially honoured as "the better things of life," and any producer is self-deceived who measures attendance without reference to the centuries of advance publicity or the legion of writers, lecturers, and teachers who serve as eager touts. People know that Shakespeare is best, and whether they know it through discovery, revelation, or common report, their hopefulness is touching, and their hunger for what is best deserves more from the theatre than successive tests of faith.

2

So much by way of exordium. The substance of my lectures was born of discontent, and it was necessary that it be expressed. I wish to propose a theatre for Shakespeare—not in the sense of a building, whether some regional Globe-restored or some national monument to the Poet-as-Hero, but in the more general sense of the auspices of production, specifically an acting company with its techniques and animating ideals. I intend to indulge in counsels of perfection and, in doing so, must assume that I know what perfection is. That the assumption is large I need not point out—the thought will occur to you spontaneously—but the time for scepticism is not yet: *imperfection* is my present theme, as always relatively safe. To those who protest that they enjoy the Shakespearean performances now available and will be robbed of a pleasure if I persuade them that they do not, I can offer only apologies and old-fashioned syllogizing. We enjoy many things, and the more fortunate we are the more things we enjoy, but unless there is a difference in the nature and intensity of our enjoyment of different things

—the play of *King Lear* and the game of darts—the difference in the nature and value of the things themselves must quite confound distinction. The question is not whether we enjoy certain things but whether we enjoy them in a certain way, and to the limit of our capacity to enjoy them, and of their capacity to be enjoyed. Theatrical events may be enjoyable simply as theatrical events, especially when the theatre itself is new to us or normally inaccessible, and occasional productions of Shakespeare may be good or at least better than others, and even the worst may contain some good thing, but all of this has nothing to do with the *best*. If we invoke the simple principle that the best plays are worthy of the best production, meaning the kind of production best for the plays, we must recognize that something is at present amiss. If what is supposed to happen when Shakespeare's plays are performed did actually happen, if they cast a spell upon audiences commensurate with the presumed potency of their magic, the fact would be so manifest as to render my challenge absurd. It would not seem slightly unsporting to inquire if the jokes won gusts of spontaneous laughter, slightly *gauche* to mention tears.

All persons roughly classifiable as idealists grow used to being taken gently aside and explained the facts of life. Concerning Shakespeare on the modern stage the remonstrance will go somewhat as follows. You complain of the polite apathy in audiences, and I understand what you mean, but it might be well if you diverted your stern gaze from the productions a moment to glance at the plays themselves. Shakespeare, we say, is not of an age but for all time, and so, in a sense, he is; but we must not let ourselves be blinded by such dazzling encomia or take our own rhetoric too literally. Not all of Shakespeare is for all time, and perhaps not all times are for Shakespeare. This is the twentieth century, and although it pains me to tell you so, there are counts against these plays quite apart from how they are produced.

Thus speaks the realist, either the friendly private monitor or, increasingly of late, the professional dramatic critic. People used to say, in voices discreetly hushed, "You know Wolcott Gibbs doesn't *like* Shakespeare," but the assumption of this witty journalist that Shakespearean producers are coping with intransigent material is no longer awe-inspiringly unique. "We must face the fact," says one reviewer after another of one disappointment after another, "that the basic fault lies in the play itself." Since all continue to display the highest regard for the author in the abstract, we gain the impression that Shakespeare would be a great playwright were it not for his plays or at least for the ones usually placed on view. This alternative possibility must be considered—that the frustrations I have so bleakly described are due not to the nature of the productions but to the nature of the plays themselves.

3

An indictment of the plays as living drama might proceed under three counts. These would be, expressed in the least compromising language, their bewildering prolixity, their archaic subject-matter, and their stultifying reputation as classics.

The characters of Shakespeare are great talkers, even those like Hotspur who claim to be ruggedly laconic, and unless one is able to gather ideas and impressions in full proportion to the number of words they use, one is certain to find them, whether one admits it or not, prolix and consequently boring. Listening to these plays is an exacting experience. They are written in a highly individual idiom of the English tongue as current three and a half centuries ago. Some of the words are no longer in use, or are in use in a different sense. The style is swift and elliptical, an unusual combination of the literary and colloquial, with a wealth of imagery drawn in part from objects no longer visible and from books no longer read. Something comparable to the haze of distance indubitably exists, challenging the vision of all and baffling that of some. I know of one youth who left a performance of *Antony and Cleopatra* in angry incredulity because the Queen of Egypt and her handmaids could not possibly have died from the bite of a "worm."

On the other hand Shakespeare's language is more than normally communicative. It was created initially with enormous power of projection, and it remains the reverse of what the more sympathetic critics of modern poetry call "private" and the less sympathetic call amorphous and imprecise. Few passages that have reached us incorrupt are inherently obscure, and even the most complex reveal the discipline of a high intelligence observing the limits of what may be intelligibly conveyed. Consequently the difficulty even of these passages tends to disappear when they are spoken by someone who himself understands them, providing the speaker is audible. One of my less literary friends has told me that he first understood what Shakespearean characters were saying in a motion picture version. "Come to think of it," he added, "it's the first time I ever *heard* what they were saying." At the theatre, from the locations he could afford, the plays had seemed to consist only of peculiarly dressed people making peculiar sounds.

It does not follow that an audible and expressive delivery of the lines solves everything for all listeners. I shall return to the point in a moment, after considering the second count in my hypothetical indictment of the plays as living drama. It usually presents itself as the obverse of the first, in a form something like this: Although Shakespeare's language is wonderful, of course, his stories and their moral emphasis now seem more than a little quaint—with so much violent and improbable action, so much idyllic love and intensity of family feeling, so much ado about chastity and the like. As a case in point, it is too much to expect the modern mind to grow greatly exercised over Othello's fancied grievance when it could not do so even

if the grievance were real. So-called adultery, after all, is amen-
able to rational contemplation, psychological as well as statisti-
cal, and suggests to civilized people nothing more sanguinary
than the divorce courts.

We might reply that the play is not about adultery, fancied
or real, but about evil preying upon innocence like the serpent
of old and the anguish of one who is led to throw a pearl away
richer than all his tribe. But that is not the point. Or we might
reply that moral sentiment has undergone a less violent
revolution than is fashionably maintained, and whatever their
course of action, most husbands in Othello's supposed situation
feel most of Othello's pangs. But again that is not the point.
We either yield ourselves to a work of art or we do not. We
are either capable of escaping our intellectual preoccupations or
we are not. The closing words of the *Iliad* on the death-rites of
Hector, tamer of horses, need not leave us cold because we are
not ourselves tamers of horses, or because the taming of horses
confers no distinction in our circle, or because the horse has
been superseded by the automobile. The standard of values of a
poet and his characters calls for sympathy, not logical analysis.

But the intrusiveness of the modern ego is a fact that must
be reckoned with. We are living in an age of a great diffusion
of superficial knowledge, and such knowledge—perhaps all
knowledge in excess of experience—is sophisticating. A great
many people find the substance of Shakespearean drama too
elemental for their tastes, and tend to view it with reserve if not
condescension. A great many others, lacking the cultivation of
these, find its language too mystifying even when audibly and
expressively rendered. Putting it crudely, these plays are basi-
cally a popular type of literature no longer accessible to a
popular type of audience; a spectator with the right kind of
heart may have the wrong kind of head, just as another with
the right kind of head may have the wrong kind of heart.
If there are factors inhibiting a full response from both of two
opposite kinds of people, the situation appears very sad—until

we happily reflect that people are not divisible into opposite kinds. Thousands triumph over their cultivation, or lack of it, and read Shakespeare's plays with delight in their language and accord with their moral and emotional burden. This also is a fact, and it renders irrelevant the charges of obsolescence. These plays are not for everyone. They are for enough to compose a qualified audience, and it is for this qualified audience that performances should be designed. If the plays can be read with enthusiasm, they could be seen and heard with even greater enthusiasm, if the performances were worthy of the plays.

But, look you, says the man of the theatre (and we come now to the last of our three counts against Shakespeare as a "living" dramatist), the standing of these plays is such that nothing we do can seem worthy of them. If we are unable to succeed with them as with ordinary plays, it is for the very reason that they are not ordinary plays. They are not greeted with ordinary expectations by audiences in ordinary moods. A performance is less a performance than an "occasion," and the spectator comes less to see the play than to see how we do the play. Consider the frightful unease of the actor as he launches into Hamlet's "To be or not to be." How can he achieve spontaneity, or seem more than the echo of a host of predecessors? His dilemma is our dilemma in little. It is all very well to say that these wares are well advertised; indeed they are too well advertised. The trouble is that the plays of Shakespeare have ceased to be plays at all—they have become *classics*.

It might be answered that all pejorative uses of the term *classics* suggest a latent devotion to mediocrity, but this is no moment for brusqueness. There is promise in the fact that the men of the theatre will admit, at least in private, that a trouble exists. Their diagnosis is natural, but not, I believe, correct. The notion that fame creates distraction, or that familiarity breeds ennui, is not supported by our general experience with works of art—with pictures, poetry, or music. That the mem-

bers of an audience have seen *Hamlet* before is no impediment
to their seeing *Hamlet* again, the play as distinct from the
production, providing the production subserves the play and
makes no separate bid for attention. Works of art are not such
that they may be contemplated more than once only under
inducement. The most literate audiences of today, incidentally,
are less familiar with *Hamlet* than were the later audiences for
which Shakespeare's own company performed it. If an actor is
tortured as he speaks its soliloquies, it is the fault of his own
misguided aspirations abetted by the tradition, or lack of tradition, in which he works. His sense that he may not simply
stand, but must sit down, or lie down, or lunge about, or turn
his back to the audience; that he may not simply speak, but
must whisper, or mutter, or shout, or must speak through
closed lips or clenched teeth, has no parallel among other inter-
preters of works of art. There are strains in the great sym-
phonies as familiar and famous as any speeches in Shakespeare,
but they seem to convey to the members of orchestras no
compulsion to start a parade or even rise in their seats. They
are not distracted, and we are not distracted. I see no escape
from the conclusion that if an audience is distracted by a
Shakespearean production as a whole—or embarrassed, or puzzled, or worst and most common of all, gradually stupefied—
the fault lies not in the classical standing of the play any more
than in its language and substance, but in the way the play is
performed.

4

One would be justified in declining to debate the potential
effectiveness of Shakespeare in the theatre, meeting doubts with
Johnsonian roundness: these are great plays and that's an end of
it. I have paused with the issue less to defend the plays than to
defend the audience—or rather to state the defensive proposi-
tion that the right kind of productions would find the right

kind of audiences even though special qualifications, of understanding, of feeling, and of tolerance for the classics, must be postulated in such audiences. Modern production is undertaken in the doubt that the plays can still stand on their own merits, or that the audiences are qualified to perceive those merits, and is marred by a determined spirit of helpfulness. It becomes increasingly apparent each year that, of all writers, Shakespeare is the one most in need of assistance, and the critic's eagerness to prevent misunderstanding is matched by the producer's eagerness to prevent mislike. He considers it feasible to design the right kind of productions for the wrong kind of audience—a Shakespeare-without-tears for those predisposed to suffer.

The peculiar and influential doctrine that the spectators will normally be such as must be compensated for seeing Shakespeare, must be administered Shakespeare with palliatives or converted to him from a deep-rooted hatred, is, like all peculiar and influential doctrines, invested with an air of righteousness. The image of the soulless schoolmaster is invoked, that villainous fellow who turns golden words to dross by telling what they mean, thus nipping away the beauty-seeking tendrils of the young—in much the same manner, presumably, as the teacher of arithmetic kills their potential love of income-tax forms. I have heard considerable confirmatory testimony about traumatic experience with Shakespeare in school (since happily nullified by well-springs of inner strength), but in my own experience of secondary education, although none of the instruction was greeted with enthusiasm, nothing was preferred to literary explication except idleness absolute. Few souls were saved for poetry, but none at all were lost.

It is chiefly in America where the educational process is revered and suspected in equal measure that the producers feel they must strive against the baneful effects of schooling. Kindred missioners in England are more apt to cite the natural deprivation of the masses. I recall how at Stratford-upon-Avon a delegation of scholars, including my unworthy self, was soothingly addressed by the director then in charge before we had seen his repertory. You will not, he said, like everything we do, but you must bear in mind that our audience consists of excursionists, and they must be given something for their penny. The words seemed benevolent and wise, until we had seen the repertory, when they were reinterpreted to mean that someone must suffer and it might as well be we. My most tearful recollection is of the opening scene of *The Tempest*, where the smallest possible ship tossing in the largest possible storm was offered in lieu of hearing or even seeing the actors. None of us wanted productions for scholars, at least in any loosely impersonal sense of the term, but it seemed possible that we were being over-victimized, and that those others about us, who had made their pilgrimage of grace to the birthplace, would have graciously accepted the poetry.

One trouble with the compensatory productions is that the excursionists are rarely given enough for their penny—not so much as they would get at the pantomime or, to return to America, at a "regular show." The inserted spectacle is rarely a first-class spectacle, the stereopticon ghost rarely a first-class illusion, the battle-scene formalized as a ballet behind gauze rarely a first-class ballet. One feels chagrined on behalf of Shakespeare, who is worthy of better spectacles, better illusions, better ballets. But even when such effects are skilfully managed, as sometimes of course they are, the chief trouble remains—the suffocating redundancy. In popular art, whatever its other defects, redundancy is as rare as dullness, and it is an error to suppose that an anti-Shakespearean audience will be unconscious of it, satisfied with it, or converted to poetry by its means. From the hypothetical point of view of this hypothetical audience, no one ruins a spectacle so thoroughly as a wordy old writer like Shakespeare.

The anti-Shakespearean audience is, in any case, only a myth, composed as it needs must be of the people who stay away. Actual audiences are only too anxious to be pleased and, failing that, to appear pleased. The things that are added unto Shakespeare leave these audiences mildly diverted, grateful for the effort expended on their behalf, and generally unresentful, but with no new awareness of literary greatness. They would be little more bored by plain Shakespeare than by fancy Shakespeare. It is pointless to argue that audiences dwindle when the plays are presented without elaborate mounting, or stars borrowed from the films. That press-agentry and "packaging" are a great power is a fact not in dispute. The argument fails to reckon with the possibility that audiences dwindle when there are no frills because there is nothing left except inferiority undisguised.

5

General charges of inferiority are rash as well as unkind, but occasionally such a charge is supported by the sheer probabilities of the case. Let us reflect for a moment on the conditions under which symphonic music is currently presented in America as compared with those of the Shakespearean theatre. Analogies between poetry and music are often loose and vexatious, the two are not the same or explicable in the same critical terms; but in one particular a play and a symphony are alike: both reach us through intermediary artists; both are designed for performance. The great difference between them makes only more remarkable the fact that I wish to point out.

Since the symphony employs the more universal symbols, and since these are set down after a more exact system of notation, one might assume that the symphony could be rendered with greater ease than the play, in a spirit of more careless assurance, and by less experienced artists. Obviously, however, everyone is proceeding on the opposite assumption. In more than a score of American cities fine symphony orchestras provide access to classical music. The least of these orchestras is more carefully organized, more continuous in its existence, more rigid in its standards, and more seriously regarded than any agency concerned with acting Shakespeare. The greater orchestras are conducted by men of international renown. They bring to their work a native gift, a technical proficiency, and a reverence for the works they interpret beyond anything known among producers of Shakespeare. The latter are energetic and versatile men and women vouchsafing to their task a few weeks of time during an interval in more exacting labours. To be chosen for the humblest place in one of the great orchestras is to be distinguished among instrumentalists. To be chosen for a minor role in Shakespeare is to be available at the moment of casting, at the lower Equity rates.

It is needless to pursue the comparison. The place of the symphony in America is no occasion for bitterness surely, and yet the lover of classical drama may well wonder what sin he is expiating that there should be such feasting for his musical neighbour and only a few broken meats for himself. That the symphony orchestras are not economically self-supporting is beside the point; we are speaking only of quality, and there is no immutable law to the effect that a Shakespearean theatre must be profitable. One further point must be noted. The great orchestras do not undertake to adorn classical music in such a way as to make it palatable to those predisposed to hate it, and yet without this effort at "popularization" classical music grows more popular every year.

It would be effrontery to ask for a score of dramatic companies as richly maintained and deservedly esteemed as the score of symphony orchestras. We may modestly ask for one. America has a wonderful array of facilities for the higher appreciation of Shakespeare: several specialized periodicals, several world-famous Renaissance libraries, many local and national societies, a large annual output of books and articles, a prodigious network of school and college courses—everything indeed except an adequate company to perform his plays. There was a time when we could look to England for productions better than our own, but we are forced to recognize, despite our reminiscent fondness for the Old Vic and the Stratford Memorial Theatre, that that time is in the past. Incredible as it seems, there is nowhere in the English-speaking world a single company or producing agency with sufficient stability, sense of direction, and inflexibility of standards to offer performances of a reliable kind and quality—pilot productions that might serve as inspiration and example. France has not one but three theatres presenting to uniformly large and appreciative audiences the French classics, with technical perfection and, more miraculously, with undiminished vitality. It is customary to view the merits of the Comédie Française fatalistically, as a sort of lucky accident. France, we say, has a fine tradition. A fine tradition is enviable, but more enviable still is the will that establishes and maintains it. A performance of Molière, like a performance of Shakespeare, is an individual thing, and may be good or bad because of or in spite of tradition. If it is a good thing, it is because someone wills it so after assessing anew the goodness or badness of the tradition. It cannot be accidentally good. Good traditions may be transplanted, as instanced by American symphony orchestras, or created, as instanced by the present-day productions of Greek tragedies in Athens. A tremendous gulf, historical and cultural, even racial and linguistic, separates the modern Greeks from the ancients, but they are performing Euripides much better than we are performing Shakespeare. The self-sacrifice of their artists in accepting professional hardship, and the anxiety of their management to do full justice to the plays entrusted to their care should have for us the force of a reproach. Our Shakespearean theatre at its best seems jaunty and frivolous in comparison.

6

I have reached the end of my lament, and my remaining lectures will be constructive. I have already, I should like to think, given support to two constructive ideas: first, that there should be a Shakespearean company committed to the idea of a completely qualified audience, so that nothing need be done to alter or enhance the effects dictated by the script; and second, that this company should meet standards of personnel and performance equal to those of the best symphony orchestras. Two questions immediately arise. What are those effects "dictated" by the script? And how, in this faulty world, is this faultless company to be recruited and maintained? The second of these questions I shall cope with in my concluding lecture, and although I shall try to do justice to other alternatives, my advocacy will be for an uncompromising professionalism. Academic Shakespeare, little-theatre Shakespeare, training-school Shakespeare, and summer-festival Shakespeare are not quite what I have in mind.

The two intervening lectures will be devoted to the first question. Granted that ballets and the like are not dictated by the Shakespearean script, just what is? There must be a stage, but what kind of stage? There must be actors, but what should these actors do? Should there be scenery or should there not be scenery? And if there is not scenery and the script reads "Jessica above," just where should Jessica be? What does the script dictate when it says "Alarms and Excursions"? Staging Shakespeare's plays presents concrete problems, and a general expression of dissatisfaction with obvious interpolations will not do. The proffered solutions must be concrete, and supported by some kind of argument other than intuition.

Before indicating the nature of my approach to a solution, I wish to point out that our one great advantage at this moment is that we are in a position to define the problem. We now know enough about the Elizabethan stage to extract from our knowledge reliable suggestion, and also we now have behind us three centuries of example in the hazards of Shakespearean production. From the late seventeenth to the late nineteenth century, the plays were vehicles for the talents of a royal succession of virtuosi. Some of these were great artists, but they viewed the plays mainly as the occasion for the display of their artistry. Their reading of famous passages was often brilliant and refined, their projection of the great roles often marvellously effective, but their tradition assumed that the texts should be so manipulated and the minor roles so faintly "filled in" by minor actors that their personal genius should appear unrivalled. The most perceptive dramatic criticism we have inherited from the long era of these kingly actors is that which protests against their imperialism. Toward the end of the nineteenth century new departures in stage lighting and other mechanisms effected a revolution in the economics of the theatre. The royal succession came to an end, and the most successful "Shakespeareans" were those who showed the most facility in trading upon the new resources of the theatre, acting impresarios such as Sir Henry Irving and Sir Herbert Beerbohm Tree. Scenic elaboration and gorgeousness became the order of the day, and again the most perceptive dramatic criticism consisted of protest.

It was in the era of Irving and Tree that William Poel began to conduct his valiant attempts to restore the plays of Shakespeare to their author. His ideals were as admirable as his knowledge and facilities were inadequate. George Bernard Shaw praised his efforts, and usually for the right reasons, but William Archer and the majority of practical thinkers did not. In the debate over the merits and defects of the Elizabethan manner as then conceived, both sides displayed the usual pride of opinion. It was assumed by the proponents that if the original manner of production could be restored, it would prove to be the right manner eternally. The reliance was upon authority, even upon Elizabethan prestige, and emphasis was placed on such things as could be most easily imitated, on Elizabethan staging rather than on Elizabethan company organization and competence. Still William Poel performed a great service and the best productions of the twentieth century, those of Granville-Barker and Bridges-Adams, have been greatly influenced by his work, while all productions have been influenced in some measure.

Poel's critics missed their opportunity to clarify the issue. Some of them conducted the discussion on a low satirical plane, and instead of trying to extract the good from the new theories, they reduced them to absurdity. If we are to remove the scenery from the stage, why not remove the roof from the theatre and let the spectators stand in the rain? Why not cast a choir-boy as Cleopatra? If we are to play *Julius Caesar* in Elizabethan dress, why not play it in modern dress and let the senators wear frock coats? There are good answers to all such questions, but unfortunately we have witnessed less inclination to provide them than to seize upon the advertising value of the reductions to absurdity. Some directors have answered, "Why not?" and regaled us with a succession of ingenious "stunts," while others have retained an underlying allegiance to the spectacularity of modern stage-craft. In the absence of any restraining tradition and in the presence of conflicting theories, Shakespearean production has become wildly experimental with the more aggressive directors as the master-minds. Some-one seems always to be getting between us and Shakespeare, first the actor-kings, then the actor-impresarios, and now the director-dictators. Perhaps we should say not some*one* but some*thing*—and that thing human egotism.

Egotism is not unknown among academic persons like my-self; hence I must try to be factual and objective in seeking in Elizabethan precedent and the twentieth-century dilemma a solution to our problem. The paradoxical nature of the problem is illustrated in the following statements. We should stage the plays of Shakespeare as they were staged in the first place, not because that necessarily is the best way to stage plays but because these particular plays were written to be staged in that way and we do not wish to change them. But if we stage them as they were staged in the first place, we will be staging them in an archaeological fashion, and they were not staged in the first place in an archaeological fashion. Hence to stage them correctly is to stage them incorrectly. I am not playing with words but seriously suggesting that in the theatre as elsewhere the style that attracts attention to itself is bad. The unusual is a psychological hazard, and we must keep in view our main end—that the attention of the audience is to be focussed upon essentials. The way out of the difficulty seems to lie in amending the first proposal. We should stage the plays of Shakespeare as they were staged in the first place, but without seeming to do so. This is the most difficult of prescriptions, because showmen do not like to do anything without seeming to do it, but I believe it is the only possible one if we are to let the greatest of all showmen again have his full chance.

We must decide what was the manner in which his plays were performed in his own time, what were the elements in that manner that are indispensable to their proper performance in any time, and how these elements may be restored in our time without creating a self-defeating distraction. We must map out the points of no-compromise, and these should lead us to the solution, to a Theatre for Shakespeare.

II. ELIZABETHAN GUIDANCE
IN THE STAGING

MY PROPOSAL THAT WE SHOULD BEGIN BY deciding how Shakespeare's plays were staged in the first place may have seemed a trifle airy. No subject in theatrical history has been more militantly disputed. Two mutually contradictory theories are at present locked in a death-grip. The older, the multiple-stage theory described in most current textbooks, maintains that the action was distributed among various acting areas, with a considerable number of episodes mounted in curtained enclosures at the rear of the projecting platform. Either of these enclosures, the so-called "inner" and "upper" stages, would, when used in isolation, function much like the furnished box-sets of the modern theatre. The newer theory, in violent opposition, dismisses the "inner" and almost the "upper" stage, proposing in their stead a number of practicable scenic structures of frame and canvas scattered about the platform and serving as the locales of a play. The term *death-grip* may be read literally: the older theory was already dying when the younger arose to challenge it, while the younger is unlikely to survive its maiden combat. And yet neither the curtained enclosure nor the practicable scenic structure is a figment of the imagination—they both existed—but to let our minds dwell on them is to misconstrue the essential nature of Elizabethan staging.

In the processes of historical as of chemical investigation we often witness the greatest surface ebullition at the moment when solutions are clearing. In recent years there has been, despite appearances, a meeting of interested minds on a number of important points, and the view that I shall present is by no means exclusively my own. In the past our great difficulty has lain less in finding evidence of Elizabethan methods than in accepting the evidence we found. We have insisted upon supplementing it with selected medieval, neo-classical, or modern data, postulating an evolutionary process that would relate the Elizabethan stage to whatever older or newer stages were more familiar to us or less shocking to our sense of decorum. We have resisted the idea of a stage *simple*, ancient as primitive dancing and modern as parlour charades, a stage truly of "scene unlimited"—unlimited make-believe.

2

Burbage's professional predecessor had been acting for over a century before a theatre was provided for him. He had, of course, a stage—a circle of turf surrounded by villagers, the floor of a banqueting chamber, a row of planks reared upon barrels or trestles in a gild-hall or the yard of an inn. When he spoke he was Everyman, and his stage was Everyplace. Symbolism was no ingredient in this drama, it was the thing itself, and it remained so—with all the world a stage, and a stage all the world. As the substance of drama became diversified and particular, Everyplace became Anyplace, or any particular place that the dialogue or action implied. In many episodes in the drama, even at its Shakespearean height, nothing at all is implied, and the place is any place suitable, just as the time is any time suitable between the time of contiguous episodes. Indoor episodes could be as easily localized by dialogue and action as outdoor episodes, and the indoor episodes increased in number in proportion to the increasing concern with indoor life. There was little need for change in staging method when the initial method was so generously permissive.

The earlier London theatres were already operating and Shakespeare perhaps already acting when Philip Sidney recorded his neo-classical distaste for the scene unlimited:

... where you shall have Asia of the one side and Afric of the other, and so many under-kingdoms that the player, when he cometh in, must ever begin with telling where he is, or else the tale will not be conceived. Now ye shall have three ladies walk to gather flowers, and then we must believe the stage to be a garden. By and by we hear news of a shipwreck in the same place, and then we are to blame if we accept it not for a rock. Upon the back of that comes in a hideous monster with fire and smoke, and then the miserable beholders are bound to take it for a cave. While in the meantime two armies fly in represented with four swords and bucklers, and then what hard heart will not receive it for the pitched field?

The note of derision should not make us flinch. It is directed at the dramatic expansiveness more than at the theatrical technique. Scaliger in France was equally derisive of a technique employing scenic backgrounds when the principle of unity was disregarded.

Speculations upon whether "Asia" and "Afric" were entrance points indicated by lettered cards are diversions from the essential fact: the episodes were obviously occurring in both "Asia" and "Afric" as well as in the "under-kingdoms"— yet all in the same place. The stage appeared to be a battlefield when the actors appeared to be battling, a garden when they appeared to be picking flowers. It transformed itself to a cave, not by visual constriction or by the actors' retreat into some constricted sub-area, but by the entrance of the dragon.

A drawing of the interior of the Swan playhouse in 1596 shows such a stage in use. In a three-tiered amphitheatre a rectangular platform extends from one sector of the encircling frame out to the centre of a yard. On the platform are three actors grouped so far forward that they are nearly in the middle of the amphitheatre. Two are standing and one is sitting on a bench. We cannot tell whether the episode is indoors or out-doors, in Africa, Asia, or England, because we cannot hear the lines. No trace of scenery or setting is visible. The vast stage stands empty except for the actors, their bench, and two permanent pillars supporting a loft-capped shelter from the sky. We can see how the actors have made their entrance and how they will make their exit. Two doors at the rear of the platform lead into that portion of the frame from which the platform extends—the only portion not given over to galleries for spectators. Even above the stage doors is a spectators' gallery so that actors are in view from all points of the compass.

We owe this drawing to the scholarly impulse of a foreign visitor to Shakespeare's London, a stranger as curious as our-selves but more blessed with opportunity. To reject or even modify its testimony would be perilous. Elizabethan play illustrations, several of which exist and are sometimes thought to suggest the use of scenery, belong to a different category of testimony: they picture episodes as conveyed by all means including the dialogue, not necessarily by the staging alone. Two additional pictures of open stages in use, although later and less authoritative than the drawing of the Swan, agree with it in showing actors upon a bare platform accessible only from the rear and overlooked by a rear gallery as well as from all other angles. One is the frontispiece of a Restoration collection of dramatic sketches, including excerpts from Shakespeare, and was evidently intended to convey to readers of 1672 a general idea of what staging had formerly been like. Both show the stage in a roofed interior so that no stage pillars appear, and both show as the means of access a split curtain instead of doors.

The pictorial evidence suggests that the only entrances to

some Shakespearean stages were made through two rear doors, to others through a split rear curtain. Additional evidence, mainly the play texts themselves and the surviving production guides known as "plots" (best studied in W. W. Greg's *Dramatic Documents*, 2 vols., 1931), suggests that entrances to most stages were made through both doors and curtain, with the curtain covering a central aperture into a backstage area occasionally opened to view for theatrical purposes. This curtained area cannot be considered a stage *per se*, no more can its existence be denied. For most of the purposes to which it was put, either of the broad rear doors of the Swan would have served, and in view of our certain knowledge that tents, tombs, and similar structures were occasionally set up on the great platform itself, any Elizabethan play could have been staged at the Swan theatre as shown, in the manner customary at all.

Only a few more points about facilities need be made. The gallery at the rear of the stage was also, like the curtained aperture, used for special theatrical purposes, so that when certain plays were performed some portion of it must have been barred to spectators. The platform itself was pierced by a trap, used primarily for the entrance and exit of spirits from the nether world, while the ceiling of the pent-house covering of the stage, at least in some theatres, was similarly pierced so that heavenly spirits might descend from the loft. Such descents were most uncommon, and Jonson's contemptuous allusion to the lowering of the "creaking throne" (Prologue, *Every Man in his Humour*) must have been as particular in its application as most of the other items in his attack. The infernal spirits were more restive, but the platform trap itself was used (for all purposes) only in a minority of plays, and in these only at rare intervals.

Curiously, the Elizabethan stage is often referred to as small, but the only one for which we have dimensions was forty-three feet wide by twenty-seven and a half feet deep. The acting area provided was therefore much greater than that provided by modern stages as normally used. It was adapted to large and mobile casts, often grouped in opposing factions or massed in scenes of pageantry. The woodwork and colouring were decorative though not illustrative, and there was nothing mean or primitive in the impression conveyed. We may turn now from its fixed physical characteristics to the way this stage was used.

3

I have re-studied in the original editions the stage directions and implied action in eighty-six plays, including seventeen by Shakespeare—all those known to have been staged by particular companies using the London amphitheatres between 1576, when the first was built, and 1608, when Shakespeare's company ceased using such structures exclusively, barring only such plays as were not printed within the same period.* The selection was made in order to avoid the confusions that might result from the adaptation of scripts to later stages or from mere editorial meddling. Most of the eighty-six texts were probably printed from scripts actually used in the amphitheatres and must be considered, collectively if not individually, as supplying unimpeachable evidence. I have studied these plays in relation to whatever external contemporary evidence is available, such as the pictures, the "plots," and the later prompt-books, as well as in relation to whatever has been conjectured about Elizabethan theatres and their methods. What I say must needs be brief, but I think it will be reliable.

At the opening of a familiar episode in *Much Ado about Nothing*, Benedick gives an order to a page: "In my chamber window lies a book. Bring it hither to me in the orchard." The words *in the orchard* set the scene. They would be super-

*The plays are among those listed as "Popular" in the present author's *Shakespeare and the Rival Traditions* (1952), pp. 343–349.

fluous if the orchard looked like an orchard. Modern dramatists do not write, "Bring it to me here in the living room."
Shortly afterwards, the cunning matchmakers intrude upon
Benedick's solitude and he says, "I will hide me in the arbour."
The words *in the arbour* are apt to send our minds seeking for
some stage object or recess that looks like an arbour, either
because an arbour would normally appear upon a modern
stage or because in some other Elizabethan play an arbour was
demonstrably employed. But just as the bare stage became an
orchard at Benedick's word, so any part of it might become
an arbour at his further word. The arbour is wherever he
chooses to stand. The probability suggested by the pictorial
evidence is supported by the text. Since Benedick continues
to speak, in lengthy asides, and since his "business" as a startled
eavesdropper is periodically described by those from whom he
fancies himself concealed, he must be easily audible and promi-
nently visible to the audience—probably standing by one of the
stage pillars now functioning as a symbol of concealment, just
as in some other play it might symbolize the tree upon which
lovelorn swains pin sonnets. In the episode immediately following, Beatrice is the hoodwinked eavesdropper, but interest is
maintained by variety. The matchmakers arrive in the orchard
first, and Beatrice is enticed to follow and hide in

> the pleached bower
> Where honeysuckles, ripened by the sun,
> Forbid the sun to enter.

We should neither assume that Beatrice hides where Benedick
"hid" nor begin draping property honeysuckles about an
"inner" stage. Beatrice need only slip in one door and out the
other, or through the split curtain if one is provided. She is
described first as running "like a lapwing ... close by the
ground to hear our conference," and then as "couched in the
woodbine coverture." Since she is given no lines like Benedick's and no implied "business" like his, she need not be

in sight at all except for her lapwing excursion and re-entry after the others have withdrawn. The action of these successive episodes presents awkward puzzles if we elaborate the arrangements of the stage, no puzzle at all if we let it stand constant and bare.

At one point in *Love's Labour's Lost* three characters eavesdrop separately and simultaneously upon a soliloquizing lover. Two places of "concealment" are suggested in the text only by stage directions bidding first one character, then a second step "aside." The symbolic possibilities of the two pillars thus presumably exhausted, a third hiding place is required. Its position is indicated by Berowne's line, "Like a demigod here sit I in the sky." Evidently he has slipped out and reappeared in the stage gallery, having yielded up his initial point of vantage to make room for a successor. The soliloquizing lover at stage centre is now amusingly bracketed by the three eavesdroppers functioning as a satirical chorus. Each of the three is unaware of the presence of his predecessor, yet clearly visible to the audience and in a good position to address it in asides. Complicated as the situation seems, it proves easily manageable if we do not tamper with the basic stage.

In *Romeo and Juliet* Romeo is followed into the Capulet orchard by his friends. There is no stage direction, but since they do not see him, he has obviously stepped "aside," just where is immaterial although probably to a stage pillar. When his friends leave, he is present to comment on the witticisms he has overheard: "They jest at scars that never felt a wound." There is still no stage direction, but his next line, "But soft! What light through yonder window breaks?" makes it clear that Juliet has appeared in the gallery. Editors, puzzled by Romeo's seeming exit before the entrance of his friends, have divided the scene in two, adding cryptic stage directions about "lanes" and the leaping of "walls." The "orchard wall" mentioned in the dialogue would have been a thing offstage, created by the words and a gesture of the speaker's hand. Since Juliet speaks from the gallery, and in a later scene Romeo descends from it after their bridal night, it has sometimes been mistaken as the setting of extensive portions of the play—those in which Juliet is upbraided by her parents, drinks the potion, and is mourned in seeming death. That such crucial scenes would have been cramped into rear recesses and insulated from the audience by a spread of vacant stage seems an initial improbability, and what actually occurred is suggested by the technique in parallel or nearly parallel situations. The stage direction "Enter Mother" after Romeo's descent by the ladder and exit from the platform does not signify the entrance of the mother to the gallery where Juliet stands. The entrance would be to the stage proper, where Juliet would immediately join her in the textually undirected fashion of Berowne's return to the stage proper in *Love's Labour's Lost*. The platform which had been the Capulet orchard as Romeo made his exit became, if one chose to think of the matter, the antechamber of Juliet as the mother made her entrance. The localization of the stage or any portion of it could be obliterated as well as established at will, even in the midst of continuous action.

This complete plasticity made it possible for characters to arrive at destinations without interrupting the play by leaving the stage: the destinations could come to the characters. Readers familiar with the instance in *George a Greene*, when Jenkin and the shoemaker of Bradford agree to fight at "the town's end," then take a few steps and say, "Now we are at the town's end," are apt to think it quaint and isolated, but it is only one of the more obvious of a number of similar instances. In the second part of Shakespeare's *Henry IV* the stricken king remains continuously in our sight and speaking as he is conveyed from the Jerusalem chamber to a bedroom. When he is conveyed back to the Jerusalem chamber, he is conveyed off-stage. Unable to believe that the mere movement of the actors upon the platform could convert the Jerusalem chamber into some other, and then banish it to a point backstage, editors have also divided this scene into two, splitting Henry's speech in the middle. It is disturbing to realize that this sort of alteration, as well as the implacable naming of specific localities for each bit of action, occurs even in the best editions we use.

Normally such localization as was established within a scene endured until the stage was cleared. Similar localization might be re-established in a later scene, but the moment the stage was cleared nothing could be assumed: the locale was erased with the departure of the actors. At one point in *Selimus* the stage is cleared *via* scaling ladders and rear gallery, momentarily localized as the walls of a town besieged. In the episode immediately following, the attackers lead in the defenders captive through the doors under that very gallery just "breached." Since we are apparently now inside the town, we are tempted to say that the gallery now represents the inner instead of the outer side of the walls. Actually, however, it now represents nothing at all—it has melted away as an irrelevance.

Our minds have tended to elaborate the façade at the rear of the stage because we have been more conscious of it than the Elizabethans seem to have been. In their production guides pegged up backstage so that the right actors would be in position to enter on cue, the point of entrance is specified only when gallery or curtained recess was to serve, or when different points of entrance were to be used simultaneously to allow for opening encounters of individuals or groups onstage—a not uncommon effect. For all other entrances, the great majority, no particular point of entrance is specified, and it looks very much as if the actors could take their choice, or else habitually entered at the door where the guide was pegged. Occasionally, of course, a particular point of entrance might be cued to the actor by the action onstage, such as the knocking upon one of the doors or a reference to it as belonging to a particular room or house, but such cues are normally absent. As we reflect on the matter, we realize that a merely customary and dramatically non-significant point of entrance would have been appropriate for most entrances upon this stage. Why cavil about *which* door, with *any* door equally implausible as an approach on a street, a road, a battlefield, to a seacoast, in a forest, and the like? The guides usually say "Enter" when the actor is to appear on an empty stage and establish the scene; and "To him," "To her," or "To them" when he is to integrate himself into a scene already established there by others. It was he who had dramatic significance, rather than the façade through which he entered.

4

It is an unhappy necessity of the discussion that we must devote most time to those parts of the stage where the least playing occurred. The major uses of the gallery have been sufficiently indicated. It served usually as an upper window, a balcony, the wall of a town, or a mere point of vantage for choral spectators of the action below. Actors in the gallery were easily heard as well as seen, as proved by the willingness of the playwrights to let characters speak there at considerable length, but it was rarely if ever used except in conjunction with the stage proper. We can understand why it originally came into use. The fables that were to be dramatized sometimes required action at more than one level. Although it was possible to accept a convention of invisibility and imagine characters hidden when they really were not, and a convention of foreshortening and imagine characters moving in a few paces to some different locale, it was not possible to imagine that they could be reached only by scaling ladders when they stood at stage level. We can understand the distinction and fix the point where the imagination would boggle.

The uses of the curtained recess between the stage doors were equally occasional and specialized, and it too was rarely if ever used except in conjunction with the stage proper. When there was to be a "discovery" or surprising *emergence* from hiding, it was deemed more effective if the actor was hidden in fact. Falstaff was discovered behind the curtain sleeping off his intolerable deal of sack, and through it Polonius was stabbed. Sometimes the curtains would part upon the recess furnished and peopled, but the device was rare, and just as the texts prove that the gallery was suitable for extensive speaking, they prove that the recess was not: the playwrights got speaking actors out of it as promptly as possible. We can see the process operating in sufficient instances to draw conclusions about the rest, even when the episode in question both opens and closes in the recess practicably localized as a study, bedroom, or the like, as in the case of Zenocrate's death-scene in the second part of *Tamburlaine*. In a number of instances one can actually count the number of lines spoken inside and outside the recess, for instance in the Induction to *The Merry Devil of Edmonton*. A familiar example may be cited in a play excluded from my test-group of eighty-six. Shakespeare's *The Tempest* is as likely as any of his plays to have been first performed in the roofed auditorium of Blackfriars rather than in one of the amphitheatres, but after the stage direction "Here Prospero discovers Ferdinand and Miranda playing at chess," the young lovers are required to speak only three lines before the dialogue is taken up by the characters on the stage proper where the subsequent action proceeds. Except in a few particulars, such as the use of *entr'acte* music which will be discussed in the next lecture, the staging practices at the later Blackfriars, at least until the end of Shakespeare's career, seem to have been little different from those to which he had originally adapted himself.

By no means do all such stage directions as "Enter a banquet," "Enter in his bed," or "Enter in his study" mean that the recess was used. If a character appeared on the platform

holding a book and candle, he had "entered in his study."
Such a direction as "Enter a maid with a child in her arms, the
mother by her asleep" (*A Yorkshire Tragedy*) seems to dictate
an opening tableau behind parting curtains, and so I should
interpret it, but such another direction as "Enter two with a
table and banquet, and two other with Slie asleep in a chair ..."
(Anon., *Taming of a Shrew*) creates a reasonable doubt. Tables
furnished with banquets, beds occupied by sleepers, even
tombs to be haunted via the trap, not to mention mere banks
where the wild thyme grew, were, as is easily demonstrable,
carried on and off the stage when occasion required. Minor
items were often transported by the actors who were to use
them: in *The Devil's Charter* even so august a personage as
Lucrezia Borgia is required by the stage directions to carry in
a chair and to carry it out again when it has served its lethal
purpose. We may assume that their *entourage* relieved kings
of the necessity of transporting their own thrones.

Since the curtained recess was sometimes used for dumbshows and tableaux vivants, probably lighted by torches, we
are apt to seize upon it and associate it with a pervasive spectacularity. Any unusual use of gallery or recess provides stage
directions so much more stimulating than the monotonous succession of "exits" and "enters" that there is a temptation to
generalize from them. Consequently the suburbs of the Elizabethan stage have received more emphasis than the stage itself.
The extent of the over-emphasis is suggested by the following
figures. In the eighty-six plays that I have mentioned as providing the best guide to the staging, forty-eight require no use
of the gallery, thirty-nine no use of enclosure whether on or at
the rear of the stage, and twenty-five no use of either gallery
or enclosure. In the eighty-six plays there is a total of 1463
scenes, with a scene defined as a piece of continuous action set
off by a definitively cleared stage. Of these only sixty-one
scenes require the use of the gallery, and only ninety the use of a

curtained recess or equivalent stage enclosure. In other words only a total of 151 scenes are involved, including many doubtful cases. In the remaining 1312 scenes the staging consisted of actors entering upon and leaving an open platform, either totally bare or equipped incidentally with a few seats, a table, a bed, a gibbet, a judgment bar, a raised throne, or the like. The exigencies of the fable dictated departures from the norm of simple platform playing, not the lure of the adjunct locations.

It must not be forgotten that even in that small minority of scenes where something other than the open expanse of platform was used, the platform itself was also used, and so frequently for the more striking speeches and action in determinable cases that we are justified in concluding that it was so used in practically all cases—including Tamburlaine's defiance of the gods after the death of Zenocrate, Faustus's evocation of Mephistopheles and descent into Hell, the choice of caskets in the lottery for Portia's hand, and the final piteous overthrow of Romeo and Juliet. No false impression will be conveyed by the statement that nearly the whole of Elizabethan drama was staged upon a bare and level platform against a neutral background. And it is not only the pictorial evidence alone that sustains the evidence provided by the texts. The setting of plays evoked no descriptions like the setting of masks; the recorded expenditures for stage equipment are not comparable in amount to the recorded expenditures for costumes; and the one inventory of the properties of a playhouse that survives is, considering that these properties served an extensive repertory, most remarkable for its meagreness.

After my painful researches I find it humbling to observe that the practical implications of such findings were known to Granville-Barker thirty years ago (*Review of English Studies*, 1925, p. 63):

The play was acted upon a stage. The actors came on the stage and went off it. That was the basis of the business. For the action certain "practicalities" would be needed. . . . But—this is the point—those things existed *ad hoc* only, and for the actors' convenience. They had, so to speak, no rights and life of their own. . . . The vision of the audience comprised the speakers and actors of the play, and such material things as by their use of them they brought to a momentary life, an apparent reality. Further than that it did not stray. Apart from the use that inner, outer, and upper stage were momentarily put to they were nothing, they were artistically non-existent. And scene after scene might pass with the actors moving to all intents merely on the current of the play's story and of their own emotions; unless, the spell broken, they were suddenly and incongruously seen to be on a stage.

There is nothing in this statement that I am able to amplify or amend.

5

We must agree, I think, that the kind of staging the Eliza-bethans used was best for the kind of plays they wrote. The seemliness of the relationships established by natural adaptation is scarcely open to dispute. Shakespeare exercised to the limit the freedom afforded by the accepted distinction between the theatrical image and the dramatic vision. His stage would not hold the vasty fields of France, but its imperfections could be pieced out with imagination. Titania the actor would be measurable in feet however few, but Titania in the vision would be measurable in inches—"The cowslips tall her pen-sioners be." Shakespeare seems to have been well enough satis-fied. He was not mocking Elizabethan conventions and tech-niques in the Pyramus and Thisbe scenes of *A Midsummer-Night's Dream*; he was mocking rather the literal-mindedness of naïve amateurs, who supposed that because moonlight and walls were mentioned in the script, moonlight and walls must be shown. In fact he seems to have been mocking us.

But it is one thing to say that the original staging was best for the plays, another thing to say we should duplicate it. The dramatic vision withers in a climate of archaeology, and one kind of literal-mindedness can be as blighting as another. Compromise we must, and our sole aim should be to compromise intelligently. We should try to decide what kind of modern staging will be least damaging to the plays.

Modern staging implies the use of modern theatres. Modern theatres, unlike the Elizabethan, separate the stage from the auditorium. Are we defeated from the start? or are the virtues of the central position of the Elizabethan stage in some measure transferable? We must decide what those virtues were. The most obvious was that the actors could be seen and heard. We should follow this lead without compromise. Our company must never perform except where the actors can be seen and heard. In most cities there is at least one theatre where the acoustics are good and the auditorium not too cavernous. No other should be engaged. If there are sections even in these theatres where seeing and hearing are difficult, no tickets to these sections should be sold. People may be willing to sit in them and the refusal to permit it may be costly, but we are not reckoning costs. Our aim is rapport between audience and play, and there can be no rapport if the play reaches part of the audience only as a rumour.

What were the further virtues of the position of the stage in the midst of the audience? I have consulted a number of professional producers on the subject, principally advocates of theatre-in-the-round, and their reply is that a stage in such a position induces intimacy and restores the ritualistic spirit of drama now banished by the picture-frame or "peep-show" stage. Discontent with the modern theatre is concentrated at present upon the proscenium arch. Our most influential dramatic critic, Brooks Atkinson, longs for the day when it will become obsolete; and at least one literary-minded psychoanalyst equates the audience huddled in shadowy isolation from the play with the modern fear of life and impulse to retreat to the womb. These are deep waters.

The exaltation of the open stage is historically and perhaps theoretically justified. It would be good if our theatre were more akin to those of the Greeks and Elizabethans just as it would be good if our dramatic genius were more akin to theirs. But to say that one restores the ritualistic spirit of drama by using a certain type of theatre is like saying one restores religious faith by using a certain type of church. So far as intimacy is concerned, it is highly questionable if it has much to do with physical proximity. There are few places less intimate than the lunch-counter or the elevator-car. Intimacy is created by a spiritual bond and a sense of familiarity, and it is now as likely to prevail where there is a proscenium arch as where there is not: many eloquent witnesses have testified to its genial presence in the old Shakespeare Memorial Theatre in the days of Sir Frank Benson. Advocates of the open stage are none too consistent in their theory and practice. It is modern lighting more than the proscenium arch that creates aesthetic distance, and considerable ingenuity is being exercised to preserve upon the experimental stages conventional electrical effects. The moment the house-lights go off and the stage-lights go on, the open stage must abandon even its physical claims to being intimate or ritualistic. There are, in effect, three transparent walls instead of the usual fourth, and one sees the play from unusual angles but not as a participant: I personally have never felt more like a peeping-tom than in the theatres-in-the-round. And with some of the more boisterous neo-Elizabethan stages, I have felt less that I was being drawn spiritually into the play than that the play was spilling out physically upon me.

The fact is that modern companies and producers want the means of enhancement of the performance, the means of subduing the audience to attention, provided by modern facilities quite alien to the nature of ancient stages. If the object is to approximate Elizabethan conditions, it could be done more nearly by using a conventional theatre and leaving the house-lights on. I am not offering this as a solution, but am suggesting rather that we cannot have the cake and the penny, and that such intangibles as intimacy and the spirit of ritual are, in any case, not recoverable by physical means. And even if the Globe with all its ways could be restored in pristine purity, as I wish it could, unfortunately it would not be portable and we do not want our Shakespearean company tied down to a particular site. We must not be deterred from using proscenium-arch stages, not only because these are the kind available—a weighty consideration—but because they offer no insuperable obstacle to preserving such values of the Elizabethan type of stage as are capable of being preserved. Providing we can see and hear, the position of the stage in the theatre is of less importance than the way the stage is used.

It does not follow that because there is a proscenium arch, an ornate frame, there must be an ornate picture. A modern stage can be as neutral and stable as the Elizabethan stage. It is an error to assume that because there was no frame for the original productions, there were no pictures. There were pictures of course, but since they were composed almost solely by the figures of the actors, they were free from distracting detail. This is the lead we should follow. We must provide the practicalities, but must not clutter the plays with competitive illustration—with objects having rights of their own aggressively asserted. Individuals have been saying this for a long time, and the fact that their words have usually gone unattended is no proof that they are not true. It is often charged that such purists do not really like the theatre, that they would prefer to read the plays, and so I feel obliged to affirm at this point that I personally love the theatre, and love theatrical scenery. The appearance of *Billy Budd* on Broadway filled my heart with nostalgic delight; I revelled in the rocking ship and the beautiful creaking of the spars. Musical comedy in all its garish splendour is my favourite form of modern drama, and I am devoted to the films. But Shakespearean drama is another matter, not because it is in any way sacrosanct but because of all that was implied in the initial portion of the present discussion.

When Benedick says, "Bring it hither to me in the orchard," Shakespeare was not writing redundantly, but an orchard setting will render the writing redundant. And that

> pleached bower
> Where honeysuckles, ripened by the sun,
> Forbid the sun to enter

will lose its force as an evocative image and become only another redundancy. The injury is not exclusively or even primarily to such descriptive passages, but, in ways that defy analysis, to the whole texture of the work. These are plays of a peculiarly full utterance adapted to, and only to, a peculiarly spare setting. To listen to Shakespeare creating Rome in a Rome already created scenically is to listen to two persons speaking at once. It is not simply a matter of painting the lily, gilding the rose, but of intrusion and obscuration such as in all other forms of artistic activity is recognized as intolerable. In this particular variety of drama the action and speech give us as much as we need and are able to assimilate. Anything more constitutes assault, and the better the décor—the more lovely and rich— the more grievous the assault. In art even more than elsewhere mere accretion is unrewarding, and the union of two good things may produce something not twice as good but half as good as either.

There is nothing about a stable and neutral stage that would strike a modern audience as odd or archaeological. We have become accustomed to the non-decoratively functional; in fact it is quite *modern*. The stage should be opened up to its widest and deepest extent, and its arrangement should remain substantially the same throughout the performance of a play. The arrangement should supply, harmoniously and unobtrusively, the facilities of the Elizabethan stage without imitating that stage or anything else in particular. Access from the wings will serve better than rear doors, and small balconies near the proscenium pillars better than a rear gallery. Since the play will be viewed at stage level by those in the orchestra seats, who, unlike those in the yard of the old amphitheatres, have paid more than the minimum fee, something must be done to prevent the masking of players in scenes where many assemble. A stepped-up rise of two or three feet in the rear half of the platform will do, and there need be no architectural elaboration.

Last year I saw *Richard II* performed upon a proscenium-arch stage arranged in approximately the manner described. Any other of Shakespeare's plays could have been performed upon it. The theatre was the Palais de Chaillot and the company was the Théâtre National Populaire. It is with chagrin that I say that, in a year spent largely in seeking out effective Shakespearean staging, I found the best in Paris, where the text had been redacted into wretched French prose, and where the director, alone of all those to whom I applied, had failed to dignify my inquiries with an answer. The fact remains that the staging so intelligently subserved the play as to make most of the other productions I had observed seem somewhat amateurish. The actors moved truly on the current of the play and their own emotions, and were not "incongruously seen to be on a stage." The facilities struck one as neither old nor new because they scarcely struck one at all. Properties were moved on and off the platform during brief intervals of darkness between the nineteen "*tableaux*," and even this small concession to plausibility was superfluous: the objects were so simple and slight that they could have remained on the stage, or been brought on and off by the actors with the stage in constant light. There was nothing barren, meagre, or colourless about the theatrical image. Colour and splendour were supplied by the costumes of the actors and the banners they sometimes bore, while the groupings formed visually satisfying as well as significant patterns. When living figures are the only meaningful symbols, one realizes what poignancy may attach to the mere position of such a symbol placed apart or alone.

About a quarter of a century ago the Shakespeare Memorial Company then under the direction of Bridges-Adams made several tours of America, and its performance of *King Lear* disproved the contention that this tragedy is unsuited to any stage. The setting, consisting of little more than background drapery, was remarked upon for its simplicity. My tribute to the setting is that I have no recollection of it apart from the comments in the reviews. My remembrance is of Lear himself, out-scorning the to-and-fro conflicting wind and rain in a storm so cruel that it could not have been produced by mechanical means; whatever the stage effects, they must have been subordinated and the sublimity of the poetry allowed to create the scene.

Fears that performances in a plain and inconspicuous setting would themselves be plain and inconspicuous derive from a failure to think things through. Contrast itself is dramatic, and we are denying the performers nothing so far as their own persons are concerned. Their make-up can be the best modern skill can devise, and their costumes opulent and "theatrical." Whatever focusses attention upon the players themselves may be accepted as good. My own feeling is that the stage-lighting of poetic drama should be less hypnotic, that is less intense and variable, than stage-lighting usually is, but I have no convictions in the matter. We need not be narrowly prescriptive even about the scene. When *As You Like It* is performed, a tree on the stage will serve better than the reproduction of a Swan pillar, but let it be just a tree and not such a one as might have borne the golden apples in the Hesperides, and let there be not so many that we cannot see the play for the forest. We shall simply assume that the stage technicians are anxious to do no more than is necessary, that they realize this is not their show and there is less danger in under-exercising than in over-exercising their various mysteries. This means, of course, that they must be technicians of the finest and rarest sort.

So long as we recognize the nature of the aesthetic problem, posed by the kind of plays these are, and so long as we assume a reasonable degree of sensibility in the audience, the right staging will be attainable. It need not await a revolution in theatrical architecture, or be confined to those few immovable structures which now, or may someday, exist. The greater challenge remains—the proper disposition upon the stage of the speech and action that constitute the play.

III. ELIZABETHAN GUIDANCE
IN THE PRESENTATION

N THE CONCLUSION OF HIS EXCELLENT BOOK on the Globe Playhouse, Mr. C. Walter Hodges admits to moments of fear that he might be a little disappointed if carried back for an actual visit. His uneasiness is understandable. Elizabethan plays show elements of, what shall we say—primitiveness, carelessness, improvisation? Elizabethan techniques of presentation must have shown similar elements. How dangerous will it be to refine upon our notions of the quality of those techniques? This much, I think, may be said: whatever their defects, the plays at their best were very good, and it seems at least possible that the presentation at its best was correspondingly good; any evidence to that effect must be viewed as admissible. Here we are confronted with an odd phenomenon. Historical perspective enables us to see that in the late sixteenth and early seventeenth century English drama, whatever its merits and defects, was the best being created anywhere in Europe. The English did not insist on the fact, indeed seemed none too aware of it, but they did insist—and foreigners were inclined to agree with them—that their theatres and actors were the best. Curiously, our timid hypothesis that the presentation was worthy of the plays is more than sustained by Elizabethan testimony.

The actors were craftsmen of the theatre, and it may be well to reflect for a moment upon the virtues of ancient craftsmanship. As we examine an Elizabethan book, we notice many imperfections—faulty pagination, careless proofreading, impression from worn type or mixed fonts, similar problems of composition tackled differently at different points in happy-go-lucky fashion. The English printers had the lowest standards in Europe, and this is a poor piece of work. Still, there is something good about it. The ink is still black, the paper flexible, the stitching secure—as if the faulty craftsmen responsible for this particular book had been shored-up by the craft itself, by the good materials it had created and they had inadvertently used. And the letterpress at least has personality. This is a *book*, not a slickly tooled artifact; it both was and seems to be something shaped by human hands in answer to human needs. This personality in the product, the mark of the human intercessor, cannot be reckoned a virtue in old printing without exalting old acting since acting is so purely a craft of human intercession. The actor's craft in England was older than the printer's and must have evolved something equivalent to good ink, paper, and stitching. The English actors, unlike the printers, were the best of their craft in Europe, and Shakespeare's plays were presented by the best of the English actors.

In the first folio collection of Shakespeare there is a list of "the principal actors in all these plays"—that is, the actor-sharers as distinct from the hirelings, the company members associated in any given year as a group of eight or ten master-craftsmen. Although the company had existed for three decades only twenty-six names appear in the list. The stability indicated by this minimal turnover is rare in the world of the theatre. Since membership in this company was the highest award for reliability and skill that the age could offer, since there were many to compete for the award, and since standards of excellence had existed for over a century, it seems more than likely that the original presenters of Shakespeare were able indeed, and that we have something to learn from the techniques they inherited and evolved.

What we can learn will not be, of course, a particular style of acting, and the question of style need not be extensively considered. In *A Warning for Fair Women*, acted by Shakespeare's company at about the same time as *As You Like it* and *Julius Caesar*, an actor makes an entrance upon the following stage direction: "Here enters Browne speaking, in casting one side of his cloak under his arm. . . ." His "speaking" begins with the following lines:

> This way he should come, and a fitter place
> The town affords not; 'tis his nearest way
> And 'tis so late he will not go about.
> Then stand close, George, and with a lucky arm
> Sluice out his life. . . .

We see now that the actor was to cast "one side of his cloak under his arm" so as to bare his sword hilt and thus prove himself intent upon murder. It is a gesture we might suppose he could have been trusted to think up for himself; probably the playwright was merely visualizing. Such directions are exceptional, but enough occur both in printed texts and in promptbooks to provide an ample list, and the indicated gestures are in general, like the above, broad and very obvious. It is my opinion that we can determine something about the style of the acting from such data, but little about its quality and effectiveness. I once undertook, as a sort of academic *jeu d'esprit*,* to define the formal nature of Elizabethan acting, intending only to give pause to those who thought that Shakespeare's verse should be spoken as conversational prose. As a person who distrusts "schools" and has never aspired to found one, I have since been disturbed to hear the article described as a bulwark of the "formalists." In the context of any discussion of acting

---

*The more factual portion of this appears in Appendix B.

styles of the past, as in an analysis of Hamlet's advice to the players, the terms "formal" and "natural" are apt to be misleading. Good acting is always the same, in that it employs persuasively the current conventions whatever they may be. Since the exact nature of past conventions is irrecoverably lost, and since we could not use the knowledge even if we had it, there is no use lingering on the subject. Certain skills and attitudes which accompanied the Elizabethan style have meaning for us and will be mentioned later on.

2

The actors were their own producers and directors, and we had best begin with an examination of the kind of compositions they essayed to transfer from script to stage. The eighty-six plays previously mentioned as providing the most reliable sampling vary greatly in length, from the brief *Yorkshire Tragedy* to the lengthy *Hamlet* and Ben Jonson's truly prodigious *Every Man out of his Humour*. The average length, the mean length, and the length of greatest occurrence of the eighty-six all fall within a range of 19,000 to 22,500 words, but the ascent is so gradual between such widely divergent lengths as 12,000 words and 27,000 words that it is impossible to say that there was any fixed standard. It has been suggested that all the longer texts must have been cut in performance, and that all the shorter ones are defective or unrepresentative, but there is no real evidence that such is the case. The five texts that are longer than 27,000 words are by Shakespeare or Jonson. *Every Man out of his Humour* actually was shorter in performance, and the others may have been also, but it seems doubtful that the plays of Shakespeare and Jonson were habitually cut. Probably they wrote at length both because they wrote *con amore* and because audiences were willing to listen to them, or to one of them at least, longer than to other men.

If there was no standard length of play, it follows that there was no standard duration of performances. The duration most frequently mentioned in Elizabethan times is two hours, and we may if we wish take the text-length of greatest occurrence, 22,500 words, and say that the Elizabethans performed such plays in two hours. But this is risky business, and it remains so even if we link the two hours with the shorter mean length or still shorter average length. It seems more reasonable to assume that the two hours so often mentioned was only a round number, especially since two and a half hours or more are occasionally also mentioned. Unfortunately we have no record of a timed performance of any particular text. We know that time was found at the end of at least some performances for a farcical dance or *jig*, and we also know that performances began about two in the afternoon and must have ended before four-thirty during the short days of mid-winter unless the concluding action was illuminated by torches. That it was so illuminated is quite possible, since there are contemporary hints of amphi-theatre performances even at night.

It is conceivable that Elizabethan actors spoke at the rate of 185 words a minute and presented a 22,500-word play in two hours, but it seems most unlikely. The philological experts are unable to tell us whether, at any time in the past, the normal rate of spoken English was faster or slower than at present, and the mere fact that Elizabethan scripts provided more speech than do modern scripts does not prove that the rate of delivery was then more rapid. Upon a non-scenic stage the speaking is bound to be more continuous even although no more rapid than upon a scenic stage. Upon the former the actor must speak to establish the setting, whereas upon the latter the actor must sometimes be silent in order to render organic the setting established by visual means; putting it crudely, time must be spent in dusting the furniture and dialing the phone. That the verbal element in drama decreases as the visual element increases is illustrated by any film scenario. William Poel and his successors have, in this department, proceeded upon very uncertain evidence, and the rumour of the speed of Elizabethan stage speech has done more harm than good. Whereas nineteenth-century actors delivered the lines too slowly, after cutting the text to the bone, twentieth-century actors are delivering the lines too rapidly for our comfort or understanding. Even if we knew that the Elizabethans spoke very rapidly, as we certainly do not, it would be as unwise to imitate their speed as to imitate their pronunciation. More significant to us than the length of the original texts is the length of individual speeches within those texts. These suggest that the actors enjoyed speaking; their eyes must have glittered as the long patches of verse appeared in the scripts. Since these are the scripts they accepted, they must have rendered the speeches with relish and rendered them as verse. Modern actors tend to flinch when they come to the long speeches, either because they want more leisure for *acting*, or because they are touched with the modern notion that all but the inarticulate are insincere. Our search for suggestion has not gone wholly unrewarded even at this early point: our actors should speak at the rate normal to them and intelligible to us, and should deliver the lines with relish and deliver them as verse.

Whatever the tempo of the speech, the performance should move rapidly. It is now recognized that there should be little loss of time in the succession of episodes, and Poel's influence here has been truly benign, but we have still something to learn from the Elizabethan precedent. The vexed problem of whether there were or were not intervals in the original performances is not insoluble. At the small private theatres which provided the *élite* with a place of refuge from the popular amphitheatres with which we are coarsely concerned, there were certainly intervals. Of the fifty private playhouse texts acted and printed within our test-period, 1576 to 1608, forty-eight are divided into acts and only two are undivided. The mere division of a text into acts, even when the points of division are marked by choral spokesmen, dumbshows, or *divertissement*, does not in itself prove that there were intervals in performance. The anachronistic assumption that act division predicates intervals has confused the issue even in the discussion in the learned journals. However, the mention of *entr'acte* music at the private theatres, both in contemporary allusions and in several of the texts, indicates that the act divisions marked in the forty-eight plays meant intervals in the performances, and we have a point of departure for an analysis of the amphitheatre texts.

Of the eighty-six plays acted and printed between 1576 and 1608 only thirteen are divided into acts, mostly by the early university wits or Ben Jonson, while the remaining seventy-three, including all seventeen by Shakespeare, show no formal division whatever. Choral spokesmen sometimes appear, but with such irregularity as to indicate that they are being used, in Dekker's words, "not when the laws of poesy do call, but as the story needs" (Prologue, *Old Fortunatus*). Even in those thirteen plays where act division appears, the authors seem sometimes only to have been asserting their academic respectability. Jonson in his *Sejanus*, most consciously "academic" of the plays written for the popular stage, calls for music between the acts; but his *Every Man out of his Humour*, also divided into acts, demonstrates that the author contemplated performance without intervals: the choral spokesmen at the act divisions discuss the exit and re-entrance of the characters in precisely the same way as they do at the scene divisions.

In the 1600 quarto of *A Midsummer-Night's Dream*, there are no act divisions. In the folio text of 1623 there are such divisions, and at the end of Act III occurs the stage direction, "They sleep all the act." "They" refers to the four lovers lying dispersed on the stage, and "act" to an act-interval. The most logical explanation is that sometime after 1608 when the King's Company acquired the Blackfriars "private" playhouse for winter use, musical intervals were interpolated into performances of a play that had been constructed for continuous presentation. Of the seven extant "plots" or production guides, one has cross-hatched lines at four points with directions calling for music, indicating that, for the performance in view, there were to be five acts divided by intervals. This guide proves a rule, because the other six provide for no intervals. Finally, when Shakespeare's company appropriated Marston's *The Malcontent* from the repertory of one of the private playhouses, the text was expanded, as Burbage tells us in the Induction, in order "to entertain a little more time, and to abridge the not-received custom of music in our theatre." This is direct information such as we receive all too rarely from the original presenters, to the effect that the performance on this occasion, as normally with this company, was to be without intervals.

To me the proof seems overwhelming that the plays of Shakespeare were performed, and written to be performed, continuously from beginning to end in the fashion of our motion pictures. The point is worth labouring for it has important aesthetic implications. Earlier we asked where Benedick hid and were able to suggest an answer. If we had asked *why* he hid, we would have had more difficulty. He is supplied no motive, but seems simply to hide for the convenience of the plot. But immediately after, Beatrice is provided a motive for hiding under identical circumstances, and the effect of the provision is, so to speak, retroactive. The effect would be lost, however, if an interval occurred between the two scenes as dictated by the act division inserted between them in all editions except the original one. Many other instances of the interaction of contiguous scenes might be offered. These plays proceed on a plane of emotional truth but factual implausibility, and it is the rapid continuousness of the action that articulates it and helps to make effectual the conventions. These plays should not be pondered piecemeal. Further, their emotional effect is greatest if the impact is cumulative and single, with the poet in constant control of the audience and governing its responses. I shall return to the point in a moment after raising a related question.

It does not follow that, because there were no intervals, there were no pauses. Pauses can be effective in any kind of discourse, and in dramatic discourse they can have expository utility. I believe that at those moments—on an average of sixteen to a play— when the stage was completely cleared to indicate a shift in time and place, there was a signal of such a shift in a perceptible pause, even when no properties were to be moved on or off the platform; and that this is the significance of the straight lines punctuating those points where the stage is clear in all seven production guides, and of the use of the word "clear" between scenes in one of the later prompt-books. The pause need not have been long. If I were to pause now for fifteen seconds, you would see that it is a considerable period— sufficient in a Shakespearean performance, if not in a lecture, to stimulate expectation without releasing attention, as well as to supply a recognized signal of shifting time and place. When the stage was cleared within a scene, as between successive encounters on a battlefield, there would have been no pause. Such punctuation of scenes would have extended the average performance no more than four minutes.

It is quite possible that modern productions, in inserting intervals and in trying to eliminate pauses between the intervals, are reversing Elizabethan procedure. We should have no grounds for complaint if there were no ill consequences, but I believe that there are such consequences. The anxiety to eliminate pauses between the scenes results in divertingly ingenious methods of altering settings, while the actors in the new scene almost step on the heels of those in the preceding one. That the scenes should not be sharply defined has even been elevated to an aesthetic principle, but the practical effects are often huddled and confusing. The ill consequences of the intervals are even more obvious. In timing a number of professional performances of Elizabethan plays during the past few seasons, I have found that the actual playing time varied from a little less than two hours for Massinger's *A New Way to Pay Old Debts* to a little more than three hours for a *Hamlet* moderately cut. There were in addition usually two intervals of ten or twelve minutes each. These seem to have been inserted on the principle that seeing the play would prove an exhausting experience, and the greatest demand could be made upon spectators while the evening was young and they were still fresh. Usually there was quite a long segment first, followed by two much shorter ones after intervals. The effect was to dissipate illusion, and to reduce the totality of impression and emotional impact of the play. The injury was especially apparent in the third short period of playing; after the let-down of the second interval it was virtually impossible in the short time remaining to restore the mood and tempo proper to the conclusion.

One may suppose that, in practice, the interval problem resolves itself into how long the English spectator can do without a cup of tea and the American without a cigarette, but such is not really the case. The majority of spectators indulge in neither delight but merely wait for the play to resume. At the motion pictures audiences tolerate continuous performances and bear up remarkably well even at double features. In the case of the shorter Shakespearean plays it might prove physically endurable as well as artistically desirable to imitate the Elizabethan method and present the plays with such inter-scene pauses as I have mentioned but without intervals. For the longer plays, perhaps for all, there might be a single brief interval at an early point in the performance so that at least the heart of the drama and its culmination would come to us intact. For the single arbitrary interval there is no precedent suggested by Elizabethan evidence, but there are a few instances among the earlier interludes.

3

I should like now to speak of the guidance supplied by the original method of staging battles, and—with apologies for the invidious juxtaposition—the original conventions governing the stage conduct of the women and the fools. One must be selective, and my selection of these three topics is the result of my observation of the areas of production that prove most troublesome on the modern stage.

Sidney's satirical allusion to the armies "represented with four swords and bucklers," Jonson's to the "three rusty swords," and Shakespeare's own well-known lament create the impression that the original staging of battles was a sorry makeshift:

> And so our scene must to the battle fly
> Where (O for pity!) we shall much disgrace
> With four or five most vile and ragged foils,
> Right ill-dispos'd in brawl ridiculous,
> The name of Agincourt.

But the company staging *Henry V* would have available a score of quite good foils, and actors who knew how to use them; we must not read the deprecatory words too literally. What is indicated by such allusions is an awareness of the danger of ludicrousness of effect, and we can be sure that the better companies avoided the "brawl ridiculous." Yet they did represent battles, and we must follow suit or else distort the plays. Productions of *Coriolanus* that omit the display of military prowess at Coriole so tip the scales against the talkative patrician that he is converted into something dangerously like a stuffed-toga.

The techniques which the Elizabethan presenters devised

recognized the impossibility of creating an illusion of mass combat by visual means. The audience did not see the battles so much as hear them. What it saw was displays of skill by two or occasionally four combatants on that small sector of the battlefield symbolized by the stage. Often it did not see even that. We think of Marlowe's *Tamburlaine* as a succession of mighty battles. Hostile groups are constantly entering with drums and trumpets to confront each other upon the stage, whereupon come alarms to combat followed by gloating speeches and the display of disarmed captives. But the stage directions make it clear that entrances to battle are exits from the stage. The only military action really displayed in the first five acts is Tamburlaine's pursuit of Bajazeth across the stage, and in the second five acts an ascent to and exit from the rear gallery localized as the walls of Babylon. This storming of the tire-house is a less common "effect" than one might suppose, and Shakespeare himself rarely employs it in his later plays. King Henry at Harfleur exhorts his followers to bear their scaling ladders once more unto the breach or close the wall up with their English dead, but since the enemy French, unlike Marlowe's Babylonians, have at this point made no appearance above, the audience doubtless saw only the departure of the scaling forces through the exits at stage level. Visual displays of mass fighting occur only a few times in all of Shakespeare's English, Greek, and Roman battles, and they seem to have consisted of little more than the "beating back" of a momentary debouchment through the doors at the rear of the stage.

Modern directors should read more literally the stage direction "Alarms and Excursions." The *Alarms* were sound-effects backstage: a gong insistently clanging, trumpets blaring recognizable military signals, then steel clashing, ordnance firing. The *Excursions* were individual pursuits and combats onstage. Involved were the principal personages, Tamburlaine and Bajazeth, Hal and Hotspur, Troilus and Diomede, and so it should be even when the combatants are not particularized in the stage directions. In the recent production of *King John* at the Old Vic, the battle of Angiers was represented by the usual patterned and somewhat embarrassing manoeuvres of supers. Falconbridge appeared occasionally but did nothing meaningful, and when he finally emerged bearing Austria's dissevered head, the audience did not quite succeed in suppressing its laughter. The battle had been so well behaved and Falconbridge had carried himself through it with such patronizing aplomb that the head of Austria seemed more plausible as a prize in a raffle than as a trophy of war.

The original actors were trained athletes and swordsmen. It is easier to use a weapon with lethal skill than to seem to do so, and the first art must be acquired first. We are not the connoisseurs of swordplay that the Elizabethans were, but the petulant honing of the blades does not impress even us, and when anything more is attempted we feel less elation than anxiety: it seems less likely that Austria is about to be slain than that an actor is about to be hurt. One might suppose that the greater "resources" of the scenic stage would allow of more convincing battles than were possible at the Globe, but in practice such proves not to be the case. It would be well to imitate the greater simplicity and greater complexity of the Elizabethan solution, with its small demand upon the stage, its large demand upon the versatile actor.

4

The efficacy of actor-training in the original craftsmen troupes is in no way better illustrated than by the success of the older apprentices in acting feminine roles. Women are immensely important in Shakespeare's imaginative world, but we notice that they exercise their influence through relatively few representatives. There are rarely more than two or three women among the *dramatis personae* although the number of men will often exceed twenty. The heroines are commonly

provided with fathers but not with mothers, and the fact has
been given considerable significance in studies of Shakespeare's
fixations, but the explanation is less mystical. At no one time
would a company have boys at the right stage of physical and
professional development to perform adequately the parts of
more than Portia, Jessica, and Nerissa, or of Cordelia, Goneril,
and Regan. Under the circumstances it was providential that
Portia was an orphan, and that Shylock, Lear, and Gloucester
could most effectively appear as widowers. There were always
enough boys to play the parts of boys (and we may notice
that small girls are almost non-existent in Elizabethan drama),
or of pages, pigmies, or the members of Titania's train, but
these were the young beginners. To play the part of a woman,
the young actor had to be near the end of his period of training
as well as unusually gifted. We have a sketch of such a youth in
Malvolio's description of Viola, conveniently disguised as a
page: "Not yet old enough for a man nor young enough for a
boy; as . . . a codling when 'tis almost an apple. 'Tis with him
in standing water between boy and man." That the scarcity of
feminine roles is due to the scarcity of qualified youths rather
than to a sense of their inadequacy is proved by the nature of
such roles as occur. *The Merchant of Venice* might well have
been titled "The Lady of Belmont" since Portia is its unifying
figure and is assigned the greatest number of lines; and although
the Serpent of Old Nile quails at the thought of some "squeak-
ing Cleopatra" among the quick comedians, Shakespeare himself seems to have been willing to let a young associate "boy"
her greatness in a terribly exacting role. The fact that only to a
few morbidly suggestible fanatics did the female imperson-
ations suggest the sinful and perverse is a tribute alike to the
healthy-mindedness of the audiences and to the ability of the
actors to make a virtue of necessity.

When we assign the roles of Portia, Viola, Cleopatra to
women instead of youths, as now we should, we must respect

the theatrical intelligence of the Elizabethans. The fact that the roles were to be filled in such a way, as well as a sense of public decorum, resulted in a kind of emphasis in the presentation that was written into the lines. Its nature—the stress upon personality and character rather than upon physique—has been analysed by two very observant critics, Harley Granville-Barker and Elmer Edgar Stoll. Their approach to the subject was widely divergent but they came to identical conclusions, that even in the love scenes the implied action precluded amorous embraces or displays of sexual allure. More actual caresses are indicated in *Antony and Cleopatra* than in any other play, but they are still astonishingly rare, and even the most casual reader must have observed that the seductive charms of the enchantress are stressed only when she is not in view.

Someone said a long time ago that pretty women had ruined the English stage. We must indignantly deny this hard impeachment, yet concede that pretty women have often helped to ruin Shakespeare upon that stage. By aggressively exploiting their physical charm, they can be just as irrelevant and distracting as other forms of scenery. A few years back the critical appreciation of a Broadway production of *As You Like It* concerned itself almost exclusively with Rosalind's legs, which competed with the play in about the same measure as the vast tree-roots over which they stumbled. In one of her early films the actress who triumphed in this peculiar way had worn a prim party dress and, mounting a living-room stairway, shyly spoken the balcony speeches of Juliet. The effect was beautiful and moving. Rosalind is different from Juliet, but not in the way that excited the reviewers. Present styles in feminine stage deportment do not fit Shakespeare. In tragedy it is more likely to be the women than the men who tear the passion to tatters. Lady Macbeth is a fierce inciter to evil, but what makes her so memorable is that she is also a solicitous wife; she was never designed to rend the air with the full-throated wails of a

Medea, and for a boy it would have been impossible. Cleopatra's physical allure, like Antony's warlike prowess, is
represented in twilight, and all the "business" suggesting the
seraglio is indescribably clumsy. We are too apt to think of our
ways as urbane, those of the Elizabethans as uncouth, but the
Shakespearean company could teach us urbanity in presenting
the symbols of womanhood. What we have to learn from
them here is the lesson of restraint.

5

And now for one of the touchiest problems of all. When I
maintain in disputes with the sceptical that a Shakespearean
play on our stage might still prove vital in all its parts, I am
often pinned to the wall with the question, "Do you think the
jokes are funny?" To this I always reply that we know whether
jokes are funny only by whether we laugh. This is not an
evasion. The nature of the comical varies with the occasion,
and is of one kind one place, of another kind someplace else.
What is laughable in the circus tent would be a nuisance and
bore in the home. What is so amusing in the pages of the *New
Yorker*, those shots at sitting pheasants filling out the columns,
even the delightful cartoons, need their own environment as
well as their own precise form. They seem to sicken and die
in a warm and gregarious atmosphere where animal spirits
flow, and if one tries to add to the merriment of a festive
gathering by describing even the cleverest, he will watch his
words lie withering in the unresponsive air. Reviewers should
recognize these truths before generalizing about Shakespeare's
"deplorable clowns."

Some of Shakespeare's humour is of such universal appeal
that it is production-proof and need not here concern us. The
difficulty enters with the routine punning and chop-logic of
the professional fools. We sometimes defend it upon historical
grounds, citing the Elizabethan fascination with language and

verbal gymnastics, but no amount of learned apology can save
the lines from falling flat, and I am inclined to think that the
defence is wrongly based. Shakespeare's word-play is infinitely
more subtle and swift in his poetic passages than in those he
writes for the clowns, and it seems reasonable to conclude that
the air of ponderous display that so often marks the latter is
owing to conscious design. The humour supplied the clowns
had to sort with the wooden lath rather than the steel rapier.
It is formal, deliberate, and owlish rather than casual and quick.
We watch mountains labouring and giving birth to mice.
Pedantic lameness is not the highest form of humour but it has
enduring appeal, and if spoken with slow unction the poorest
jokes are the funniest. Not all of the lines of the clowns are in
the mode described, but the occasional telling thrust is set off
by an obtuse and fumbling norm.

The error of modern actors is to assume against their own
convictions that they are engaging in brilliant repartee. They
try to make the lines sparkle and snap in the fashion of modern
comic routine, or else try to deliver them in the rubrics of duly
endorsed sagacity. Their accompanying antics are usually the
reverse of amusing. There is the "broad" mode, assumed to
be lustily Elizabethan but too convincingly imbecilic, and the
harlequin mode, involving hopping about the stage and perch-
ing tailor-fashion on furniture. The tradition established itself,
together with the parti-coloured tights, in fairly recent times.
We do not know just how Shakespeare's Kempe and Armin
conducted themselves, but we know that they succeeded
Tarleton as the funniest men in England. What Shakespeare
set down for them was designed to tap the well-springs of their
native drollery. Here lies the cue to salvaging the laughter in
Shakespearean clowning. We must recognize that the role of
Launcelot Gobbo was then, as it is now, more difficult to fill
adequately than the role of Shylock. The *lines* did not carry it
then, and the *lines* cannot carry it now—we dare rest content
with no one short of a master. A Kempe or an Armin is a

rarity in any age, but mere realization of that fact will serve us as a warning: we must not complete our casting until we have found a Gobbo who can make us laugh.

6

In discussing presentation I may seem to have concentrated upon marginal matters. The reason for my selection of topics is not only that the company that does well in the areas treated is likely to do well in the rest, but also that routine problems of presentation do not lend themselves to specialized discussion. The bulk of any Shakespearean play consists of two or more characters conversing in our presence in all veins from casual or affectionate concord to passionate discord verging on physical violence. Occasional characters appear alone and commune sometimes with us and sometimes with themselves. The movement of the actors and its timing, the way they group themselves and accompany their words with significant gesture, will be determined by technical principles not exclusively applicable to Shakespearean drama. These principles must be applied by experienced professionals, and my only suggestion is that the professionals in question should, like the original presenters, function only as theatrical technicians and not as literary critics.

I have observed that whenever the presentation of a Shakespearean play is treated discursively, the subject-matter soon ceases to be theatrical technique and becomes Shakespearean criticism. This is equally true, if not equally ominous, whether the discourse is by Granville-Barker or Wilson Knight. Mr. Knight explicitly states that the production itself should be a criticism of the play—that is a projection of the director's interpretation of it. Quite apart from whatever opinion I may have of the critical powers of him or any other possible director, my advocacy is for an attitude precisely the reverse. I believe that the great problem for the director is how to avoid imposing himself upon the play and the audience, and that his only safe course is to blank out from his mind any over-all critical conceptions. Earlier I said that the audience should not be permitted to contemplate a Shakespearean play piecemeal. Now I should like to add that those who present it should be permitted to contemplate it in no other way. Their concern should be only with each individual speech and action as it appears, and their guide only the script. To maintain that the production under such circumstances would have no coherence or unity is to deny that coherence and unity have been provided by the author. No further binding elements are needed than the appearance and personalities of the actors who play the individual parts. The danger is in over-direction and sophistication. There is nothing in the script of the first scene of *King Lear* to suggest that Cordelia is incurring "tragic guilt," but those who assume that Cordelia has read the play, as they have done (along with some out-moded criticism), so that she is aware of the consequences of her honesty, may be tempted to transform her righteousness to self-righteousness and make the subsequent calamities glance back upon her as their author. Such a reading of the play has been aptly attributed to the error of omniscience, but the point is that it is a reading. The presenters should stick to the writing and let us form our own conclusions. We all know what happens to productions of *Hamlet* when directors have read of the Prince's "Oedipus complex," and illustrations of the intrusiveness of the critical approach could be multiplied indefinitely.

Let me return to the original presenters. They were craftsmen of the theatre, and happily nothing more. They were actors, and although theirs was a craft of intercession, it was the type of intercession proper to actors. They wrote no criticism, even when they offered to the public the plays of their fellow in collected form. Their business was to follow the directions written into each line of their parts with all their craftsman skill and not to meddle with the whole. They would have been ready enough to accept suggestion from Shakespeare, but the intercession of someone who was neither poet nor actor, that is a critic, or a director, or a critical director, would have seemed very strange to them. An imitation of their innocence would save their modern counterparts from being whimsical and heavy-handed.

A few words may be added about certain attendant features of their art. Our film makers have formulated a rule to the effect that one should not convey by words what is fully conveyed by action. Since it is a rule of economy, I believe it is a good one. Its corollary was probably observed by the Elizabethan actors. Because Shakespeare's plays convey so much by words, it would seem advisable for actors of any era to be wary of inventing superfluous "business." They should do only what their situation in any particular episode, or the emotion implied in any particular line, compels them to do. The right actors will be rightly compelled. It should not be offensive to point out that the virtues most frequently commended in the original actors were good voices, good diction, and graceful motion. When one commends these virtues now, he is always misunderstood. It is assumed that he wishes actors to be mere elocutionists. What makes an actor is something else—temperament, personal magnetism, imagination, emotional suppleness, a mimetic instinct, all those qualities that give acting its inner life and authority and us a sense of conviction—but no actor was ever handicapped by a good voice, good diction, and physical grace. Shakespeare's poetic dramas were composed, and would only have been composed, when these virtues were current and respected. They can only be properly presented when these virtues are again current and respected. All the points of no-compromise in this inquiry guide us one way—to the acting competence of the presenters. It is in recognition of this fact that my concluding suggestions will be made.

IV. PROPOSED SOLUTION

NE WHO MERELY LECTURES UPON SHAKESPEAREAN production is an armchair strategist enjoying the usual immunities; he must defer at least to the hardihood of those who brave the heat of actual combat. High courage and good intentions lie behind many productions, some of which are financed, directed, and performed at the cost of real personal sacrifice. Expressions of disapproval from civilians behind the lines are bound to sound carping and ungrateful. My thesis is not that those spontaneous efforts now in evidence should be stifled or rigidly standardized but that they should be provided with exemplary leadership. The hardihood, the good intentions, the self-sacrificing energies, not to mention the genuine talents often engaged, are worthy of the best channelling our reflections can suggest. As I briefly review present auspices of production, my purpose is not to seek flaws but to demonstrate that the fundamental flaw is the same in all instances, and that any improved auspices of production must be designed to eliminate this fundamental flaw.

The productions towards which one is apt to feel least charitable are those at present commercialized at the Old Vic and Stratford Memorial theatres, England, or sporadically presented in the West End or on Broadway as the vehicles of various "stars." They are in general less good than they have been in the fairly recent past, and one feels that an opportunity has been missed; one can understand the necessity of the economies in casting but not the reliance upon "effects" since the historical appeal of places or the prestige of individuals, not to mention Shakespeare's own drawing power, has provided almost captive audiences. My impression that seeing Shakespeare under such auspices is seldom anything more than an empty rite was sufficiently indicated in my opening lecture. One feels better disposed towards the less publicized work of the repertory and road companies still heroically active in suburban and provincial theatres, even in English pubs and American grange halls. Unfortunately our approval must be on moral rather than artistic grounds. In these days of films, television, and radio, "stock" no longer thrives and we may as well admit it. A sapping process is in constant operation, with the more talented troupers lured into less arduous and more profitable activity, and with those who remain depressed by a sense of defeat.

What of the one additional kind of normally commercialized Shakespearean productions, those under the aegis of the motion picture industry? I think the opinion is fairly general that in the last five or ten years, while stage-Shakespeare has been declining in merit, film-Shakespeare has been showing improvement. The reason may be that the film makers have come to recognize that, so far as they are concerned, the only possible resource is respectful adaptation. There is nothing wicked about adaptation. As Shakespeare levied upon the literature of the past, our times have a right to levy upon Shakespeare. His was a poetic medium, and he transposed miscellaneous works into dramatic poetry. Those who work in a pictorial medium have the right at least to try their best to transpose dramatic poetry into pictures. If spectacle is to alternate with speaking, the text must be ruthlessly cut, and the best of the film versions are those which have tended to recognize the alternation principle. We lose inimitable poetry, just as when Dickens is similarly adapted we lose inimitable prose, but what remains is worthwhile to the extent that the adapters are masters of their medium and honestly intent upon reproducing the spirit of the work which lends their own creation its initial prestige. The picture may be truer to the original than the stage production of the uncut text, if in the latter the retention of the lines is the only form of deference to the play. The trouble with the screen versions is less that the lines are cut than that so many of those retained are very poorly read; the fact that we can hear so clearly magnifies the fault. The inadequacy of the actors is again our main complaint.

The increasing success of Shakespearean films may help the Shakespearean theatre recognize its proper function. Pictorially it cannot compete, and it should need less urging upon historical grounds to abandon its ill-advised attempts. What it has as its peculiar possession is the living actor and his living voice—it should make the most of them. Some of our most engaging Shakespeare is performed at the colleges and universities because of the enforced simplicity of the mounting as well as the academic responsibility of the coaches. If one wishes to represent the wild sea-waves with the mechanical ingenuity of an Inigo Jones, there isn't enough money. If one wishes to represent them with a dancing chorus, the Professor of English will object. The weakness of academic Shakespeare, needless to say, lies in the acting. Usually there is one young man who is not only a born actor but whose voice and diction put the efforts of the faculty to shame, one young woman whose shy bravery is exactly right, but the descent from these heights is precipitous.

Academic Shakespeare shades more or less subtly into summer-festival Shakespeare. It would be ungracious indeed to adopt a tone of austerity towards the latter. What better way of motivating an automobile tour than to pick as one's destination San Diego, California; Ashland, Oregon; Antioch College,

Ohio; Stratford, Canada; or Stratford, Connecticut? One feels
that the hopeful days of Chautauqua have come again, is stirred
by the spirit of local enterprise, and mingles with pleasanter
people than one would find at Saratoga or Atlantic City. Also
occasionally one sees better Shakespeare than has been available
in New York, London, or the parent Stratford. Unfortunately
it is far from a sure thing.

In the summer of 1954 the four festivals listed above which
were already operating played to a total audience of nearly
197,000 people. The Oregon Festival has survived fourteen
seasons, and a particular tribute is due to the consistent sense of
responsibility of its director, Angus Bowmer. It is possible that
out of such activity will emerge productions of general artistic
significance, but there are obstacles that must be recognized.

Most of the festival theatres are experimenting with open
stages, to a greater or less degree conceived of as Elizabethan.
Apart from the fact that all are flood-lighted, it is questionable
if any are preserving the values of Shakespeare's stage in significant measure. The first thing we notice about the neo-
Elizabethan stages (and to those of the festival centres may be
added those at Hofstra College and the University of Illinois
as well as those formerly created by the admirable enterprise of
Bernard Miles in St. John's Wood and at the Royal Exchange,
London, and of Nugent Monck in the Maddermarket Theatre,
Norwich) is that all of them alter the shape and reduce the size
of the platform. None has ever provided the forty-three by
twenty-seven and a half feet of rectangular area which is
dictated by the only known Elizabethan precedent. The reason
is that, at some of the theatres, "inner" and "upper" stages
have been so extensively used as to render a large platform
intrusive, while, at *all* the theatres, seats have had to be provided at the expense of the platform because there is no galleried
amphitheatre. It would appear impossible to restore the physical conditions of the Elizabethan playhouse unless they are

restored entire. While some of the stages are preserving more of the Elizabethan values than are others, none are preserving so many as was done on the proscenium type of stage I have described at the Palais de Chaillot, where there was not only a more spacious platform but also less stage distraction. A plethora of pillars and steps, together with multiple and surprising means of access to the playing space, sacrifices the value of unobtrusive stability. Steps were originally introduced as a means of preventing the masking of actors on a full stage, but they are exercising an increasing fascination in their own right. Even college performers are abandoning the auditorium in favour of the library entrance, and it seems to be assumed that a tragic victim looks convincingly dead only if lying head down on a flight of steps.

Festival methods of staging should not be condemned because they are not truly "Elizabethan." They must be judged on their own merits, both in fairness and in recognition of the fact that valuable procedures have been hit upon in many fields of activity as a result of misapprehension. My criticism of the "more-or-less open" staging is that, in some of the theatres, important action is cramped into rear recesses and insulated from the audience by bare platform; in others, the action in general seems diffuse, fidgety, almost ant-like; and in all, there is an atmosphere of experimental novelty. We should not be so convinced of the value of experiment as to forget that all purposeful experiments are failures except the last, all purposeless experiments disintegrative. At the more effervescent centres, the spirit of stage experiment has been accompanied by an even greater than normal spirit of literary meddling. The Capulets have been represented as moors, Petruchio as a cowboy, and the weary like. One can sympathize with the impulse to combat audience apathy, but when interest is sustained by making us say, What next? what is next will never be Shakespeare. One thing must be said for nineteenth-century productions before the days of either Irving or Poel. The staging methods, although ponderous and inappropriate, were neither overwhelmingly impressive nor restlessly experimental. One knew what to expect in the theatre one attended. Once the familiar old sets had rumbled into place, they could be taken for granted and attention concentrated upon Mr. Kemble, or Mr. Kean, or Mr. Booth. The old prompt-books reveal by their underscorings and marginal notations how such actors strove for full understanding and perfect emphasis, while some of the old reviews show that their readings were analysed with a subtlety no longer appropriate. It matters little how lines are read when the characters themselves are scarcely recognizable and the play as a whole converted into a "romp." I shall return to the point later on.

Neither the type of stages in use nor the midsummer night's madness sometimes in evidence is so dampening to our hopes as something else. The open stages could be effectively used, and sometimes are, the direction governed by modesty and good taste, and sometimes is; the big problem still remains. It is when festival Shakespeare is at its best that we are most conscious of obstacles to further progress. The companies are necessarily defective. The name Stratford is limited in its magic, and neither the centres so-named nor any of the others are in the enviable position of Oberammergau—or of the Bach country in Pennsylvania. What makes the Bach Festival an event in the world of music is the company of native performers created and sustained by a long local tradition; the privilege of listening to them must be earned by assiduous application and long waiting. At the Shakespeare festivals the performers must be recruited each year, and considering the difficulties of the process, it is remarkable that their success is as great as it is. They are usually students or professional beginners, performing as a group for the first time. The demands of repertory performance (and the ambitiousness of some of the repertories is astounding) are added to the demands of a new and difficult medium. The seasoned professional actor sometimes imported as the star is not necessarily seasoned in Shakespeare, and even if he were, the defects of Broadway casting practices would only be reproduced.

Shakespeare has written no one-man or one-woman plays. Burbage may have excelled his fellows, but the remaining eight or nine master-craftsmen and ten or fifteen journeymen and apprentices could not have been dimmed by his blinding light. The parts written for the lesser actors are often difficult and always important. The plays demand a distributed excellence in acting such as the star system cannot supply, an *ensemble* proficiency such as newly recruited and hastily rehearsed groups of enthusiasts cannot even approximate. The centres operating in connection with training schools are endeavouring to place the emphasis nearer to where it belongs, but the Shakespeare we want must be presented by actors already trained, and these schools will be drained of talent in exact proportion to their success in developing it. The festivals then, although one hopes it may prove otherwise, seem not destined to supply the type of performances that may set a standard. We trust that they will continue to flourish and add in their high-spirited way to the amenities of summer travel, but their wider function will probably be confined to the developing of individual actors for some other type of company.

2

I come now to my proposal. It seems to me useless to discuss a theatrical project except in relation to actual theatrical facts. When new plays with small casts can rarely make a financial go of it, old plays with large casts cannot do so without artistically ruinous concessions in the area of the minor roles. We may wish that the facts were different, that "show business" were not what it is, but there is less likelihood of its changing than of our being able to adapt our project to it. The perfect auspices for the performance of Shakespeare would be now, as in his own day, a permanent repertory company composed of the finest professional actors alive. Such is unobtainable, but something of the tradition, atmosphere, *esprit de corps*, and *ensemble* proficiency of the non-devitalized repertory company might be successfully simulated. Ours would not be truly such a company, since membership and tenure would be externally controlled, with authority residing elsewhere than among the actors. One of the present-day conditions we are regretfully recognizing is that the acting profession has relinquished its rights in management. It would resemble such a repertory company in the permanence of its over-all identity, and in its commitment to a certain way of doing things. Membership would be for the limited term of a single year with renewal viewed as a reward rather than a right, and with contracts guaranteeing nothing in the way of particular roles. The directors, like the actors, would be enlisted for limited but renewable terms, so that the composition of the company would be completely plastic, with the question of who was to participate at any given time governed solely by artistic considerations. If one asks how in the world the right actors and directors can be persuaded to accept conditions like these, the answer is simple—by offering them more money and prestige than they could get elsewhere.

Before proceeding further, I had better discuss the matter of financial support. The present day purchases under regular market conditions present-day products, in the field of entertainment as in any other. It is natural that this should be so, and we must not be confused by the fact that a modern film, a modern musical, occasionally even a modern play can be produced to financial advantage. It is no damning criticism of the general audience that its interests are mainly contemporary and that the idiom to which it most readily responds is the purely familiar. *Oklahoma!* is still able indeed to pay its own way, but if it is revived three centuries from now, it will probably need a subvention. We take for granted the existence of the economic handicap so far as the classics in general are concerned. Art galleries do not *pay*, libraries do not *pay*, and symphony and opera do not *pay*. Why should Shakespearean drama be barred from the privileged list? Its record of survival on the open market has been remarkable indeed, but the time for support has come.

The actual sum needed may be dismissed with the statement that it must be sufficient and therefore quite large. Mention of a large sum of money is apt to make the commercial producer look up. "At last," I can hear him say, "you have said something *practical*. Give me sufficient means, and I will give you good Shakespeare." But I am by no means assured that he would. The tendencies now predominant suggest that the money would be misspent. The costliest productions recently on display have been among the poorest, their adventitious success dependent mainly upon the advertising value of big names or of production accessories either mechanically novel or air-borne by the ton. How do we know that, with unlimited means, brass bands might not supplement the sixty-piece orchestras, or that the stage might not cease simply to turn on a pivot and begin to revolve on an axis, with conduits piping in the music of the spheres? In the hands of the restlessly ingenious the less money the better, and we can count upon a stage that at least stands still.

The money must be spent not upon buildings, or advertising, or scenic and musical accessories, but upon what every turn in the present investigation has revealed as the true indispensable—the actors. It must be spent upon salaries, and upon many instead of a few. This is no glamorous proposal, and the source of the funds must be discussed. A tax upon the Shakespeare industry, including the properly pro-rated incomes of publishers, hotel proprietors, and lecturers like myself would be poetically just, but the proceeds would be too variable and difficult to collect. A government subsidy, although there are good European precedents, would not do on this side of the Atlantic. Our national legislators are not only mercurial, but they have an odd sense of proprietorship about the things they buy with our money, and we should not like to see productions shaped to the alternative tastes of the ins and the outs. Municipalities and local philanthropists are our benefactors so far as classical art and music are concerned, but a theatre for Shakespeare should belong to no one community.

The best answer, I believe, is the type of foundation established by bequest to supply a large permanent endowment for a particular kind of activity. Such foundations have become a unique and invaluable feature of the pattern of American civilization as a result of both economic and moral forces, and they will continue to multiply so long as Americans continue to grow wealthy, to resent confiscatory inheritance taxes, and to feel democratic gratitude and goodwill. It has been pointed out that as more and more of the traditionally charitable functions are assumed by government, the new foundations will have no choice but to adopt cultural aims. It seems to me by no means unlikely that a theatre for Shakespeare will one day be endowed. Large fortunes have already founded great libraries largely or wholly in Shakespeare's honour, and the gentle rain will drop again. We must only hope that the future benefactor who is destined to link his name in perpetuity with one supreme will show some imagination, and think in terms of a theatrical company instead of a theatrical building.

Please follow me in a swift transition and suppose that the endowment has been secured. There will, of course, be trustees—of the usual integrity and dignity, but also of sufficient cultivation to make them stern wardens of the ideal of

actor-centred, poetry-respecting classical productions of Shakespeare comparable in finish to the work of the Comédie
Française. They will be good enough at distinctions to recognize that plays traditionally labelled "romantic" may still be
classically performed. The trustees will appoint as foundation
secretary the best available administrator knowledgeable in the
world of the theatre, and the latter will supervise a permanent
executive staff. We need concern ourselves here only with
those officers responsible for recruiting. These must be expert
judges of acting and directing, as well-informed, mobile, and
ruthless as the talent scouts of professional baseball and
amateur football. Their field of operation will be all parts
of all English-speaking lands where there is any theatrical
activity, including the valiant frontiers. The majority of their
choices will probably be from that strata of artists strangely
designated as "supporting actors" in plays and "featured
actors" in films. They will be less interested in the artists whose
public ascendency is such as to constitute a threat to *ensemble*
excellence. Often the established "star" is so proficient at self-
projection that he projects himself out of Shakespeare; in any
case his aura would be a hazard, and the present Shakespearean
greats will be of more value to us as directors than as performers. That there is a shortage of properly qualified actors is
beyond dispute, but it is absurd to suppose that the shortage
is too acute for the formation of one good company.

We need not be worried about the ability of the company
to obtain the services it wants. Since it is not operating on the
star system, the non-specification of roles in the contracts will
not be a limiting factor. At least one year of prosperity and
participation in a great enterprise is guaranteed, and theatrical
casting in general has nothing nearly so good to offer. The
organization is at a financial advantage to compete, and its
prestige will soon match its advantage since such is the way
of the world. It will be recognized as unique, and membership

for at least a season will lend a cachet to any acting career. About twenty-five or thirty fine artists backed by a thoroughly efficient and solvent command will be our theatre in any given year.

Three plays a season will be enough, let us say a history, a comedy, and a tragedy. As the circus goes into training quarters in the fall and comes out in the spring, our company will go into training quarters in the spring and come out in the fall. The rehearsals will be preceded by coaching in the language of the Renaissance, spoken and unspoken, until all members of the company are placed upon something approaching the advantageous footing of the original presenters. Audiences will never have the uneasy sensation that any of these actors is handling his first rapier or making his first bow, or does not know precisely what his speeches mean. There will also be drill in such fundamentals as diction and metrical speech, but no one will be starting from scratch. The recruiting has supplied not only fine actors—true actors, not mere elocutionists—but also masters of the spoken word.

There will remain more time for actual rehearsals than is ever devoted to them under conditions now current. To the later rehearsals summer visitors may be admitted, but the sole aim of the directors will be to bring the company to peak for its winter tour. This, of course, is a touring company. It will present a play a week during a three-week stand in each of eight or ten large centres of population. In addition its annual repertory will be telecast and filmed. Although a film of a stage production is neither a motion picture nor a play, it can be a fine documentary for use in the schools, better than anything of the kind now available. The telecasts are for the millions who have no access to theatres. At the regular performances there will not be enough seats for all who will soon wish to attend, but this is as it should be. Seeing these performances will be a reward for Shakespeare enthusiasts of the necessary alertness and enterprise: the seats must be ordered far in advance. If the foundation is embarrassed by finding that its tours and telecasts pay, it can distribute its surplus funds as grants-in-aid to academic and summer-festival companies. In sports this is known as *farming*, but it raises regional standards of skill and is a boon to regional fans.

3

To make such concrete proposals upon an academic occasion may seem inappropriate, even a little coarse, but I am relying upon your tolerance. In the interest of our causes we seize what opportunities are generously offered. Proposals must be made sometime somewhere—"blue-prints" as they now are called— and mine is not wholly lacking in academic features. Blue-prints have usually to do with such things as road systems and the distribution of thermo-nuclear reactors, but I am prepared to defend mine in rivalry with these on the basis of both usefulness and feasibility. The proposal needs the filling in and correction that would be suggested by a systematic study of subsidized or controlled theatrical activities such as Metropolitan Opera, D'Oyley Carte, the French National Theatre, and the like, but I do not believe that it can be dismissed out of hand.

Let us see what can be said against it. It postulates foundation support, a large permanent endowment, and no endowment is at present in sight. The sum solicited in aid of the Shakespearean centre in Connecticut is relatively modest and yet proving difficult to come by. It is my opinion that sums may be too modest to inspire any confidence that they will be effectual. Recognition of the fact that financial support must be constant and adequate has the virtue at least of abating confusion and of reducing many problems to one. We are more likely to get what we want if we say in italics that it will have to be liberally paid for. That it will actually be so paid for, by someone sooner or later, is far less chimerical than that it will come into existence in defiance of economic facts.

There may be the further objection that my proposal is simply too neat, and would not work out even if funds were available. Carefully calculated procedures are poisonous to the spirit of the theatre. Theatrical art needs the stimulus of danger and uncertainty. Its normal atmosphere is that of the thin margin and impending crisis. It snatches its great victories from defeat, and makes its most triumphant crossings over the knife-edge of probable disaster. One can imagine proponents of this view dismissing my theatre for Shakespeare *a priori*: it would be all very safe, all very sound, and all very dead.

There is something to this objection, but it should come only from those who have been walking the knife-edge of disaster and successfully getting across, with success measured in terms of artistic significance rather than financial survival. If we scrutinize the objection, we discover that it is self-contradictory. It points to danger in deploring the enervating absence of danger. Of course there is danger for our theatre, the most stimulating of all—the danger of artistic failure. At the first sign of stodginess in any season, all bookings will be cancelled and the company paid off and dispersed—that should be crisis enough, and the kind that only this management could afford to supply.

The actors and directors of our theatre will feel the necessary competitive impulse. They will be competing with fine productions past and to come, with their own achievements and those of other artists. They will be interested in improvement rather than in change for the sake of change, and the problems of effective presentation will become more challenging as they are brought gradually into focus. The problems cannot even be recognized so long as the mode of production remains erratic and roughly inventive. The effectiveness of a certain gesture or the stress of a certain word will seem as important to actors and spectators in this Shakespearean theatre as in the Salle du Luxembourg. And why not? The remaining corpus of English dramatic literature provides room enough for romping and the display of Saxon vitality. Perhaps consciousness of details diminishes as artistic perfection approaches, but we are further on our way to this unconsciousness when the details are small than when they are large. When we find ourselves discussing the propriety of introducing a chorus of nuns into *Measure for Measure* instead of how Isabella reads her lines, no challenge has been met and no step towards perfection taken. The productions will not be dead. They will simply not be galvanized into appearing alive, and so will come alive indeed. As effective techniques are recovered, the difference in successive productions of a play will become less obvious but artistically more exciting.

4

Someday there will be an endowed theatre for Shakespeare, worthy of him and its angelic founder. Unfortunately we must wait, and the question arises of whether anything can be done in the interim. Perhaps until we can get what we want by purchase, we can get something more nearly resembling it by moral pressure. Shakespearean producers are not really happy when they hear the judicious grieve, no matter how they may rationalize their resort to sleights and stratagems. I think we should grieve more often and more audibly. In the first decade of the present century the loudest journalistic acclaim was being given the productions that were most stunning. They were judged by the eminence of the star, the size of the investment in scenery, and the proposed length of the run. The negative voices were few and somewhat muted. Sidney Lee was saying that the more homely productions of Frank Benson were generically superior, and Professor Raleigh was saying, with unaccustomed acerbity, that the men of the theatre should not use Shakespeare as a platform for self-display. One would have said that no one was listening, but in the next decade came the productions of Granville-Barker and thereafter the golden age at Stratford. It is my guess that between 1912 and 1932 there were individual productions better than any since Shakespeare's own day. Perhaps I am stressing the influence of academic censors in excess of the evidence; still I believe as a general principle that the times when our voices seem to have the least carrying power are the very times we should keep on talking.

My recapitulation will be brief. Although I believe them based upon reasonably adequate historical evidence and reasonably objective observation, my specific suggestions about staging, presentation, and company organization are naturally open to criticism and subject to discount. My underlying assumptions, however, I think must stand. These are, first, that there is no theatre at present doing justice to the plays of Shakespeare and our own capacities for aesthetic and emotional response; second, that the theatre of Shakespeare's own time offers guidance in improvement if we quietly emulate the essential virtues of its procedures but do not capitalize upon the novelty of overt imitation whether accurate or impressionistic; and third, that the *sine qua non* of a first-rate theatre for Shakespeare is a first-rate company of actors, and although the maintenance of such a company means financial subvention on an unprecedented scale, an interim improvement in productions would result if energies were concentrated upon improving the acting skills available instead of devising subterfuges.

Such has been my subject if not my theme. If my theme should be described as a plea for Shakespeare pure and undefiled, I shall not protest. Unless we take the plays upon his terms we are not taking them at all. We owe our chance to read what he actually wrote to those editors who have resisted the perennial impulse to improve the text, whether by bowdlerization or its reverse. If it had not been for their integrity, the plays would by this time have been eroded into insignificance. There must be a corresponding resistance to altering their emphasis when performed. Rather than tailor them to twentieth-century tastes, we could more honestly, decently, and profitably stick to twentieth-century plays. The ingratiating words "significance for our times" can cover a lot of unconscious fraudulence. If the significance of these plays for our times is only what manipulators in our times happen to think significant, we are certain to lose the best thing they have to offer us—the reminder that our frightening and mysterious universe remains beautiful if seen through wise and religious eyes. What precisely are the advantages of Shakespeare impure and defiled?

In asserting that the plays are better than anything directors can do to them, I am also asserting that they are better than anything critics can say of them. The impulse of the latter to link their creative efforts with Shakespeare's is human and forgivable but no different essentially from other kinds of name-dropping. There should be a chance to escape these frustrated creators by returning not only to pure texts but also to pure productions. I am by no means exempting persons like myself when I deplore the intrusiveness of the middlemen. In teaching Shakespeare, one begins with hopes of how much good one may do and ends with hopes of how little harm one may do. Perhaps it would be best just to read the plays aloud. But one reads so badly! Then is born the vision of perfect productions—Shakespeare speaking for himself with most miraculous organ.

APPENDIX A. THE ROLE OF THE SHAKESPEAREAN PRODUCER

IN SHAKESPEARE'S TIME THERE WERE NEITHER dramatic critics nor theatrical producers in the present sense of the terms. Criticism consisted of approbation or disapprobation, usually moral and expressed in general terms, or of argument upon such technical principles as the unities. No one felt called upon to mediate between the playwright and his auditors—to exhibit the beauties, analyse the subtleties, or explain the *meaning* of a play. Similarly, production consisted of converting the written word into the spoken word, the implied theatrical action into real theatrical action, by methods so simple and standardized as to be relatively neutral. A text might be revised between one series of performances and the next, but there is no evidence that by processes other than textual, plays were consciously reshaped upon successive revivals.

Today, of course, all this is changed. As we read Shakespeare, a hundred critical voices are whispering in our ears, voices of the present, voices from the past, many wise and harmonious, others simply insistent, but in either case introducing into the reading experience a factor other than the poet's page and our own susceptibilities. Our protection is that the voices are so many and various as to blend into an indistinguishable murmur

almost as unobtrusive as silence. Against the producer, however, we have no like protection. We cannot attend a performance except in his personal custody. We cannot listen to
Shakespeare except to the accompaniment of his single and
penetrating voice. He is, alas, the one inescapable critic.

One need be inimical to neither critics nor producers in
order to recognize that both, and especially the latter, are prone
to rashness and are often too aggressive for our good. What
follows is in essence a plea to the producer for self-restraint,
based upon a reminder that from an historical point of view he
is with us only upon sufferance.

That the modern "producer" (in America the "director" or
"producer" *cum* "director") had no counterpart in Elizabethan
England is perhaps best indicated by the fact that no word was
created to designate his role. Even those most nearly in his
authoritative position, such leaders of the juvenile troupes as
Edwardes, Farrant, Mulcaster, Westcote, Evans, and Pierce
retained only the designation "master," deriving from *schoolmaster* or *chapel-master*. Since the repertories of the companies
governed by these men consisted mainly of plays written by
themselves or by poets closely associated with them in playhouse management, they can scarcely be equated with the non-
writing, non-acting specialists of the present, and none of them
gained a reputation from mere adroitness in guiding plays
through rehearsal. Evidently such guidance was not considered
"creative" or particularly difficult. Even in the court masks,
where the staging was sufficiently complex to evoke a tech-
nology of artificial lighting, and where a diversity of specialized
skills, poetic, musical, choreographic, cried out for co-ordination, we hear nothing of a "producer" as distinct from individual creative artists. The personnel of the Revels Office was ac-
tively engaged, but as Jonson distributes "credits" through the
printed texts of his early masks, he commends only such men as
Masters Giles and Herne, for the choreography, Master

Ferrabosco, for the musical score, Master Jones, for the scene and costume designing, and himself for "the invention of the whole" (*Hue and Cry after Cupid,* 1608). Presumably Jonson or Jones, or both, came nearer to filling the role of "producer" than did any staff sergeant of the Master of the Revels.

It is the adult professional troupes such as originally performed Shakespeare that must chiefly engage our attention. As functions in their theatres became sufficiently differentiated, words were found to designate those who performed them: *player, poet, house-keeper, sharer, hired-man, musician, gatherer, tireman, book-keeper, stage-keeper.* The list, although nearly exhaustive, is short; yet short as it is its items overlap. For instance, the *book-keeper* (custodian of scripts, and prompter), who was a *hired-man,* seems also to have functioned, at least in some companies, as *stage-keeper* (stage-manager and -caretaker). It has even been suggested that he was the counterpart of the modern producer or director. If so, his directing hand must have been tentative indeed, since the actors under his presumed direction were his masters, employing him at six shillings a week and never, so far as the records indicate, admitting him to a place as sharer in a company.

No doubt the book-keeper's or stage-keeper's authority was only minor, that tyranny in petty matters which all of us must suffer from faithful aides. Someone else must have distributed the parts of a new play and decided whether it was worthy of new costumes. These would have been the core considerations in any Elizabethan "production," and the signs are unmistakable that decisions were reached by the actor-sharers as a group or by one of their number delegated by them. The latter, possibly Shakespeare as poet of the company, possibly Burbage as its principal actor, possibly some lesser member distinguished only by a time-tried levelheadedness, may thus be envisioned as, in a sense, the "producer" in the Chamberlain's-King's Company. Since it is difficult for a group to make a series of minor deci-

sions in concert, it is possible that this hypothetical producer
may have arbitrated points of stage strategy. The simplicity of
Elizabethan stage strategy has probably not yet been adequately recognized, but the present argument is independent of
such an opinion. Whatever the emphasis and effects desired,
and whatever the technical means of achieving them, and whatever the system of delegating immediate responsibility for the
application of these means, the ultimate authority was vested
solely in the actor-sharers as a group. In the circumstances the
great arbiter would be the script. It would be the only agency
for keeping a company of equals in step, and for ruling out
repercussive distortions. The distortions of particular roles,
with their disturbing effect upon other roles, are possible only
in the type of production where some individual has an over-
riding vote. The Elizabethan script might be altered in rehearsal, but between that script as finally endorsed and the
acting company, no agency intervened; hence, between the
playwright's original conception and the audience, no agency
intervened except the acting company. It is for this reason that
we may justifiably deny the existence of a "producer" in
Elizabethan times.

The intervention of the actors themselves may seem, in the
present context, too important to be lightly dismissed. The
playwright's conception was not established and preserved as a
thing holy and entire, and the lament of Dekker is by no means
unique in its age:". . . let the Poet set the note of his
numbers even to Apollo's own lyre, the Player will have his
own crochets, and sing false notes in despite of all the rules of
music" ("Lectori," *The Whore of Babylon*, 1607). Nevertheless
the tendency would have been to defer to the script, for the
reason already given—the necessary conservatism of a democratic system of company organization—and for the additional
reason that there was no occasion for doing otherwise. As free
agents, the actors bought and staged only such plays as they

wished to buy and stage. That the method of staging itself was not of a type calculated to alter the character of the text provided by the author cannot here be argued in detail, but it must strike anyone that, within a specified period, staging and stage-writing must be truly complementary. When plays were printed, their stage directions were rarely amplified. Laconic though they certainly are, they were nevertheless deemed a sufficient guide to visualization. It is safe to say that reading Shakespeare and seeing Shakespeare in the theatre were, in his own times, less disparate experiences than they have been at any time since. In the theatre the experience was not a different experience but the same experience intensified.

So long as the King's Men endured as an actor-sharer company, that is until 1642, the tendency, despite a few decorative interpolations like those in *Macbeth*, and the introduction at Blackfriars of *entr'acte* music and perhaps occasional experiments with scenery, was to perform the plays of Shakespeare in a manner established by tradition rather than to strive for new effects and altered emphasis. We may guess that between Shakespeare's death and the closing of the theatres the impulse to *produce* rather than simply *re-perform* the plays was, at any rate, only fitfully in evidence since there was not yet any authoritative individual to implement the impulse. The testimony of the Restoration prompter, John Downes, although unreliable in details, proves the existence of a conservative ideal. The part of Henry VIII, he avers, was "right and justly done by Mr. Betterton, he being instructed in it by Sir William, who had it from old Mr. Lowin, who had his instruction from Mr. Shakespeare himself." And again, concerning the performance of the role of Hamlet, "Sir William (having seen Mr. Taylor of the Blackfriars Company act it, who being instructed by the author, Mr. Shakespeare) taught Mr. Betterton in every particle of it. . . ." (*Roscius Anglicanus*, 1608, pp. 21, 24.)

The ideal, of course, did not survive the early Restoration

period, and, curiously, the most conspicuous agent in its dissi-
pation was that very Sir William mentioned by Prompter
Downes. Sir William Davenant may with justice be called the
first Shakespearean "producer." The present author has been
inclined to deprecate the obloquy heaped upon Davenant in
view of his real love of Shakespeare, but, like all things, "real
love" must be judged by its consequences. As Professor Odell
wittily put it, Davenant "loved Shakespeare so much he could
not leave him alone," whereas Killigrew, the rival playhouse
manager, who was relatively indifferent to Shakespeare, was
inclined to stage the plays unaltered (*Shakespeare from Betterton
to Irving*, 1920, I, 24). The paradox is not without significance.
All of our contemporary producers profess, and most of them
no doubt have, a *tremendous love of Shakespeare*.

Of course there were factors at work in the Restoration
treatment of Shakespeare more potent than the mere personal
inclinations of Davenant or any other single individual. These
factors were two in number: first, the substitution of a mana-
gerial for an actor-sharer system of company organization,
with a consequent substitution of dictatorial radicalism for the
democratic conservatism previously noted; and second, a
spreading hiatus between the plays and the audience because of
the passage of time and the changing character of playgoers.
Precisely these factors have been operating ever since in giving
us "productions" rather than performances of Shakespeare.

We may without inappropriateness pass directly from the
Restoration to the present day. The mid-twentieth century, at
least in the English and American theatrical worlds, is more *like*
the Restoration than like any other era. The adaptations, from
Davenant's to Cibber's, are no longer so frequently subjected
to condemnation (which would now sound somewhat hypo-
critical), and the most notorious of them, the operatic *Tempest*,
was of late considered worth the trouble of a revival. Suffice it
to say that Davenant, from his day to ours, has been succeeded

by a long line of "producers," actor-managers and others,
aided at first by such authors as Tate, aided at last chiefly by
stage technologists, but early or late, relying mostly upon their
own fertility. Some of these producers, notably Garrick,
achieved their most erratic effects while purportedly restoring
Shakespeare to his "true and original form." Such claims might
be traced as a subsidiary tradition in post-Restoration production, with a concluding survey of the activity in twentieth-
century "Globes."

No one would wish to deny the virtues of experiment or to
dissipate the golden aura, not always spurious, hovering over
three centuries of Shakespeare in the restored English theatres.
Fine things have sometimes been done and great joy sometimes conveyed. It is not my present business to linger with
these things, or with the fact that playhouses and players have
an enticing glamour of their own quite apart from whatever
they may do with or to a poet's dreams. Austerity of tone must
inevitably accompany my attempt to make my point. My point
is this: the best readers of Shakespeare, those who have gone
to the theatre with the highest expectations, have long been
the ones most cruelly disappointed there, and the responsibility
lies at the door of the producers or the complex of production.
Charles Lamb's indictment of Shakespeare-in-the-theatre is
wrongly based, but his statement about the productions he saw
(which only "brought down a fine vision") is the simple truth
about *the productions he saw*. Coarser sensibilities than his were
intervening between Shakespeare's text and himself. Mr. Eliot
says essentially the same thing (*Elizabethan Essays*, p. 16):

. . . I know that I rebel against most performances of Shakespeare's plays
because I want a direct relationship between the work of art and myself,
and I want the performance to be such as will not interrupt or alter this
relationship any more than it is an alteration or interruption for me to
superpose a second inspection of a picture or building upon the first. I
object, in other words, to the interpretation, and I would have a work of

art such that it needs only to be completed and cannot be altered by each interpretation.

Unless one is committed to a faith in Mr. Eliot's infallibility, one must see that his error in laying his charge against the kind of plays these are equals Lamb's in laying his charge against performance rather than particular performances. At any rate both Lamb and Eliot, strange bedfellows, attest alike to the unfortunate accidents that so consistently befall Shakespeare's plays en route to us as spectators.

The features of a few recent productions and the attitudes of a few contemporary producers may be placed in evidence. In the 1953-54 production of *All's Well that Ends Well* at the Old Vic, the King of France was treated as a comic character. The phenomenon is indicative of the haphazard nature of theatrical "influences." In the undergraduate days of the present writer it was the custom among students to take turns in repeating the gnomic utterances of their academic elders to a chorus of artificial yawns. The exercise at the time seemed finely rebellious, sophisticated, and indescribably funny. In England, where for better and for worse, the literary and undergraduate worlds are more interpenetrable than elsewhere, a like custom must still prevail, judging from a scene in Christopher Fry's *The Lady's Not for Burning*, where several youths yawn away the wisdom of the world. From Fry to Shakespeare must seem a logical step—in the *All's Well* of the Old Vic the wisdom of the King of France was greeted by the exaggerated yawns of his young courtiers. By this (and less subtle means) he was converted into a figure of fun.

Now it is true that Shakespearean characters are susceptible to much diversity of evaluation. There is, however, a limit to its permissible range. No sane observer has ever mistaken Bottom for a dignitary or the King of France for a buffoon. That the actual words of Shakespeare were being repeated on the stage of the Old Vic is immaterial—the *producer* was composing this portion of the play. To proclaim that the language of Shakespeare is nowadays less frequently cut and no longer revised is to rejoice in a technicality.

The example will suffice for all those instances in which the producers consider the comedies insufficiently comic and the tragedies too tragic, and while honouring Hamlet's injunction to let the clowns speak no more than is set down for them, feel free to recruit their number—most commonly by transforming into a Polonius any available oldster in the dramatis personae. A different kind of directorial "touch" was illustrated in the 1953-54 production of *A Midsummer-Night's Dream* at the Shakespeare Memorial Theatre. The creatures of the fairy kingdom were made not comic but grotesquely sinister, especially Puck, who moved about either in somersaults or with a repulsively simian roll, like nothing so much as a stunted Caliban. True, Elizabethan fairies were commonly conceived of as malicious, but in this particular play by this particular author they are conceived of as reasonably genial. Puck, as a matter of fact, has struck generations of observers as not a little puckish, and when he ceases to be so, and when his co-spirits lose their charm, we are not compensated either by the evidence of research on Elizabethan fairies as a class or by the opportunities seized by the costume-designers.

It is invidious to point in this fashion to productions which err only in being typical. There is place for exploratory treatment surely, perhaps place for productions of precisely this kind; the calamity is that it is the only kind now available. The two have been cited because they were sponsored by the semi-official companies of Shakespeare's London and Shakespeare's Stratford, where if anywhere one might look for deference to the poet's conception. At both theatres a system of guest producers has been instituted. Since the same persons alternate as guests, forming literally an interlocking directorate, it is difficult to see the purpose of the system unless it be to allow time for the persons concerned to approach each new production with a new stock of notions.

To cite the views of particular producers, when these views are shared by all, is even more invidious than to cite the qualities of particular productions. I can only say that I have been guided in my choice by the desire to represent the three main types of apology by the three most distinguished spokesmen.

Mr. G. Wilson Knight, although relatively inactive in the professional theatre, is so influential as to be truly formidable. He may stand as spokesman for the *interpretive* producer. Mr. Knight believes that a Shakespearean production should be shaped to subserve the central philosophical idea of the play as conceived by the producer (*Principles of Shakespearian Production*, 1949 ed., pp. 35-36):

Interpretation will always be a development in a new medium of some central idea of wholeness in the original; grasp of that central idea forcing a vital re-creation. It is the same with production.... The producer should be able to hold the play in jig-saw bits in his mind, to sort them all out, to build with them and recreate the whole from understanding of its nature. Such understanding gives him full powers to cut, adapt, even on rare occasions, transpose, according to circumstances; he has to consider his stage, his company, his audience.

Everything in fact, one is tempted to add, except his author. Mr. Knight does not tell us who is to vouch for this authoritative "understanding of its nature" or how we may distinguish between the play's idea and the producer's idea of the play. By rebuilding with "jig-saw bits" an interpreter may convert his idea of a Titian into his idea of a Picasso, and however masterful the original painting, the *contaminatio* may be merely vulgar. To those producers who would cut, adapt, and transpose in the happy assurance of their "grasp" we can only repeat Cromwell's cry to the prophets of the Kirk intoxicated with spiritual fulness: "I beseech you in the bowels of Christ think it possible that you may be mistaken."

Dr. Tyrone Guthrie, who has been kind enough to discuss

these matters with me (with an admirable absence of cant), may speak for the *vitalizing* producers. Although he defended the Old Vic treatment of the role of the King of France, on the basis of the diversity in Shakespearean criticism, implying that since nothing is certain nothing is ruled out, his more serious view was expressed in a different connection. After professing admiration for the productions of Granville-Barker, he added that it would nevertheless be death just to go on in Granville-Barker's way. With this attitude one must have much sympathy, but whereas growth is evidence of vitality, change is not always evidence of growth. No one would advocate the servile imitation of anything, or a completely static tradition, but it remains true that all good productions of a particular play must have a great many features in common. On more philosophical grounds it may be argued that the work of art with which we are concerned is the play rather than the production, and the play is a *fait accompli*. It cannot be equated with a living organism. The organism can change; the play can only be changed. It cannot be *vitalized*; unless it retains its initial vitality it can only be animated. Fortunately those who have had in their custody the works of the master painters have felt no inclination to vitalize them. The analogy is not so pointless as it may seem. Although the Shakespearean plays are in a different category of art in that they invite manipulation, the manipulation was originally designed and might still be designed merely, in Mr. Eliot's phrase, to complete them; and although they are in the happy situation of having in their reproducible texts a more indestructible fabric than paintings, they can be at least *momentarily* destroyed.

Miss Margaret Webster's well-known views may be cited as those of the popularizing or *persuasive* producers. After passing adverse judgment, frequently acute, upon one of the works advocating production in "the original manner," she says (*Shakespeare Quarterly*, 1952, p. 64):

It would be of great interest to scholars and students and some sections of
the public who were already Shakespeare "convertites"; but in my view it
would have the reverse effect on the large majority of audiences who, at
any rate in the United States, have to be persuaded that Shakespeare is
anything but a dead "classic" without modern urgency or personal appeal.

To this we can only respond with anguished questions. Just
what performances are now available to the "convertites"—
those who need no persuasion and find it insufferable? Are *their*
tears not wet, *their* sobs not audible in the night? Hath not a
convertite senses, affections, passions? If you tickle them, do
they not laugh? If you poison them, do they not die?

The views of the producers have not been fully and fairly
represented, or adequately combated. It is enough to show
that they exist. Presumably when there were no producers,
there were no views, and the plays of Shakespeare were vital
and persuasive in their own right, as well as self-interpretive.
To the extent that they seem to us still so we must either shun
the theatre or be encumbered with well-meant assistance. One
may venture to say that the hiatus between plays and audience
previously mentioned can be closed only by the effort of
individual members of that audience. For those who cannot or
will not make this effort there are modern plays to be seen.
All producers shudder at the idea of productions merely
archaeological, and properly, but it must be pointed out that
selecting for performance a three-hundred-year-old script
tends toward the archaeological and one should be willing to
abide by the consequences. There is no use in pretending that
the old play is a new play. It may be true that there is now no
audience for the old play, but it is difficult to see how this may
be determined unless it is occasionally performed.

The line that has been taken may seem unsympathetic.
Nothing has been said of the producer's many troubles—with
large and costly casts, theatre overseers and subventors, journalistic critics, the absence (or presence) of "stars," and the

inexperienced younger actors, conning blank verse with one eye while watching with the other for emissaries from the West End, Broadway, or Hollywood. Let the quality of current productions be attributed to these troubles instead of to any cause suggested by me and the fact remains the same—that the quality is low. No one is compelled to produce Shakespeare, or to subscribe to the dubious principle that it is better to do a thing badly than not at all.

When all is said, however, even though they may with justice be considered the Davenants and Cibbers of our age, the producers are the ones with whom our hopes for immediate improvement must abide. We cannot summon Shakespeare to write modern plays or to modernize his own. We cannot reassemble the Elizabethan audience to exert upon twentieth-century performances those pressures that shaped both texts and performances in the first place. We cannot, unhappily, revive actor-sharer troupes with the traditions and competence of the King's Men. Since we must rely upon producers, we might profitably point out to them that their task is even more difficult than they think. A Shakespearean producer should be as reverent, knowledgeable, and technically expert as the conductor of a great symphony orchestra. He should either refuse to work with unqualified actors or else undertake to qualify them—in one way by concentrating upon their voices, articulation, and physical co-ordination the attention now directed towards their costumes, scenic background, and business, remembering that such elements in an undertaking as are least tractable may also be most important. He should know more about Shakespeare's language and frame of reference than the professors, and more about Shakespeare's theatre than the builders of models, not so much to imitate its methods as to understand their effects and to avoid a single-minded devotion to some rumoured aspect. At the same time he should regard the anxiety of the professors and model-builders to get the record straight with tolerance, and as relevant as his own conscience. Finally he should be a hopeful kind of person and assume that if he achieves the best, it will be appreciated, even in the United States, thus imitating Shakespeare's attitude in the unpromising purlieus of the Bankside.

APPENDIX B. ELIZABETHAN ACTING

THE ELIZABETHAN STYLE OF ACTING IS DISCUSSED nowhere in the four volumes of *The Elizabethan Stage*, and the word *acting* itself is missing from the subject-index. It is as if Sir Edmund Chambers would crown his generosities by leaving us a playground—one precinct free for untrammelled guessing. The sport is active, and two teams are discernible on the field, but the teams are not playing with each other: they are not defending their own inferences or attacking those of their opponents. The purpose of the present essay is not to end the game but to organize it—at least so far as that can be done by one who enters a game not as a referee but as a player. The most conspicuous Shakespearean criticism of recent years is based largely upon assumptions about the style in which the plays were originally acted, so that even a partisan discussion of these assumptions may prove useful. What follows is an attempt to define two alternate styles of acting—formal acting and natural acting—then to attack the case for natural acting on the Elizabethan stage and to defend the case for formal acting.

As spokesman for the believers in formal acting, Miss Bradbrook may be selected:

This is the general consensus of opinion on Elizabethan acting. There would be comparatively little business, and gesture would be formalized. Conventional movement and heightened delivery would be necessary to carry off dramatic illusion.[1]

[1]M. C. Bradbrook, *Elizabethan Stage Conditions* (1932), p. 109.

A murmur sounds on the opposing side that such is the *general consensus of opinion* only among those who share the opinion. The murmur grows louder when Miss Bradbrook illustrates:

Joy was expressed by cutting capers. In *Charlemagne*, when Ganelon the Senecal man is banished, he receives the news with a caper to show how little it affects him. Two more messages of unfortunate news are brought and each one elicits another caper. The tradition of such violent action is behind the most celebrated scene of *The Broken Heart*.[2]

One may concede that "Joy was expressed by cutting capers," should read "Joy was expressed by cutting capers in *Charlemagne*," but Miss Bradbrook has no fear of overstating her case.

As spokesman for the other side, Mr. Granville-Barker may be called upon, a formidable contender because his fine criticism lends error, if error it be, an alluring guise:

Shakespeare's stagecraft concentrates, and inevitably, upon opportunity for the actor. We think now of the plays themselves; their first audience knew them by their acting; and the development of the actor's art from the agilities and funniments of the clown, and from formal repetition or round-mouthed rhetoric to imaginative interpretation of character by such standards as Hamlet set up for his players, was a factor in the drama's triumph that we now too often ignore.[3]

This is a convenient passage because it expresses so succinctly so many hardy assumptions. It assumes that "formal repetition" is bad acting whereas "imaginative interpretation" is good acting; that Hamlet's advice to the players advocates "imaginative interpretation"; and that there was a development of the actor's art within the Elizabethan period amounting to a change in kind rather than an improvement in quality. Nowhere, I think, in the writings of Mr. Granville-Barker and his co-believers, is there a definition and illustration of Elizabethan acting equivalent to my quotations from Miss Bradbrook.

[2]M. C. Bradbrook, *Themes and Conventions of Elizabethan Tragedy* (1935), p. 25.
[3]H. Granville-Barker, *Prefaces to Shakespeare*, First Series (1927), p. xxiv.

Mere archaeology seems to be against them, and although they think what they think, they speak cautiously in the presence of the schoolmasters. Premises may be judged by conclusions, and the conclusions of a considerable number of writers (as represented by their criticism) leave us no alternative but to take such phrases as "imaginative interpretation" to indicate a belief that Shakespeare was originally acted much as Shaw is acted today.

The terms *imaginative* and *interpretation* can, of course, be applied to formal acting if we mean only that the actor has sufficient imagination to understand what his lines mean, and sufficient expressiveness of voice to convey that meaning to the auditors. In this sense all acting worthy of the name, formal or natural, is *imaginative interpretation*—and so also is all good reading aloud. Theoretically, if such interpretations are perfect, ten different actors will speak an identical line in identical fashion: Lowin will speak it precisely as his predecessor Burbage spoke it, and Burbage will have spoken it precisely as Shakespeare intended it to be spoken. But such is not what Mr. Granville-Barker means by his phrase. In another passage he speaks of an actor dissecting a part and reconstructing it. In other words the actor uses his imagination and applies its own products. He does not reflect, he refracts. His "imaginative interpretation" is what he puts into the part, not what he, like another, must take out of it. He "creates a role." The latter expression is modern, not Elizabethan. I do not believe it would have occurred to the Elizabethans, or that it would have been appropriate in their day. The phrase "imaginative interpretation" has the vicious propensity to mean opposite things. In the present essay it will always be placed in quotations and used in Mr. Granville-Barker's sense.

It will be necessary to clarify our terms. Natural acting is the logical alternative to formal acting. To illustrate a detail of behaviour of the natural as opposed to the formal actor, I shall quote a portion of Elena Riccoboni's description of the "new" manner of Michel Baron, disciple of Molière:

In my opinion M. Baron, generally speaking, is an excellent actor. He always listens to his fellow-actors, a thing to which, as a rule, actors pay little heed, and his attention is accompanied by such movements of face and body as are required by the nature of the speeches to which he listens. When speaking his voice is real conversation.[4]

Compare the above with a passage from J. Cocke's "A Common Player," written in the year before Shakespeare's death: "When he doth hold conference upon the stage; and should looke directly in his fellows face; hee turnes about his voice into the assembly. . . ."[5] No one would care to build a case upon Cocke's remark, but his word *common* means "typical" and does not exempt such actors as Alleyn and Burbage, whose method —not skill— was probably quite typical. If the whole of Riccoboni's description could be quoted, the distinction between formal and natural acting would appear explicit, but the brief extract is suggestive. Natural acting strives to create an illusion of reality by consistency on the part of the actor, who remains in character and tends to imitate the behaviour of an actual human being placed in his imagined circumstances. He portrays where the formal actor symbolizes. He impersonates where the formal actor represents. He engages in real conversation where the formal actor recites. His acting is subjective and "imaginative" where that of the formal actor is objective and traditional. Whether he sinks his personality in his part or shapes the part to his personality, in either case he remains the natural actor.

The distinction between the two kinds of acting is not that one is conventional, the other unconventional. Both are con-

[4]Quoted by K. Mantzius, *A History of Theatrical Art*, IV (1905), 241. For the conflict between the old and the new manner, see Tilley, "Tragedy at the Comédie Française, 1680-1778," *MLR*, XVII (1922), 362-380.
[5]Ed. E. K. Chambers, *Elizabethan Stage*, IV, 255-257.

ventional, but the natural actor simplifies and exaggerates within a wide range of choice whereas the formal actor simplifies and exaggerates by prescription. The distinction is not between emotional and unemotional acting, as Mr. Granville-Barker sometimes implies. A natural actor may simulate emotion which he does not feel, and a formal actor may feel emotion which he may seem, to the sophisticated spectator, to fail to simulate because of the pattern in which his acting is cast. In an otherwise excellent article Mr. Granville-Barker ascribes a change in the Elizabethan method of acting, and consequently a revolution in English dramatic history, to "... the great discovery ... that an actor deeply moved himself, could move and entrance the motliest audience...."[6] But the most emotional rendition of a play that I have ever witnessed was in a classroom, where a maiden lady read from her book, with eyes so tearful and hands so tremulous that twenty boys marvelled at the spectacle. What was Hecuba to her or she to Hecuba? Emotionalism is never a "discovery"; it is by definition accidental and occasional; it may not be used as a principle in identifying an art form. Let Cicero testify: " ... on the stage I myself have often observed the eyes of the actor *through his mask* appear inflamed with fury...."[7] (The italics are mine.) Emotionalism, apparently, was in evidence on the Roman stage, but it neither banished formal acting nor stimulated, as Mr. Granville-Barker implies that it should, the creation of great drama. The attitude that emotional acting and plays worthy of it are virtually inextricable can only be described as curious. The display of emotion noticed by Hamlet was evoked while his actor was reciting lines parodying bombast. The distinction between formal acting and natural acting is not, strictly speaking, a distinction between old and new.

---

[6]H. Granville-Barker, "A Note upon Chapters XX and XXI of *The Elizabethan Stage,*" *RES,* I (1925), 60–71.
[7]*De Oratore,* II.xlvii (Bohn's Classical Library, pp. 274–275).

Acting on the stage of Æschylus was formal, but acting on the cart of that Greek stroller, whoever he was since he appears not to have been Thespis, may have been, for all we can prove otherwise, natural. Formal acting is as old as ritual and natural acting is as old as the skingame; natural acting is as contemporary as the Theatre Guild and formal acting is as contemporary as the ballet. Finally the distinction is not between bad acting and good acting—but I shall come to that later.

That formal and natural acting may meet through an infinite series of gradations, that what may seem natural to one age may seem formal to the next, is true but is not available as an avenue of evasion. Baron was recognized as a revolutionary by those who had seen his predecessors. There *is* a point of cleavage. Our problem is, did Burbage and Alleyn act like Baron or like Baron's predecessors? Or, to attempt to establish our distinction where we need not rely upon descriptions, did the companies of Burbage and Alleyn act like students of Stanislavsky or like the performers in Italian opera? I use the work *like* to indicate similarity in kind, not quality, and I am not discussing totality of effect. I am willing to jeopardize my cause by mentioning Italian opera. I trust that I am justified in assuming that "imaginative interpretation" implies natural acting as I have defined it, and indicates a belief that Elizabethan acting resembled, in kind, that of the Stanislavsky school.

My first task is to examine the evidence upon which a belief in natural Elizabethan acting is based. Since Hamlet's advice to the players is rubricated by the believers, I must quote it in spite of its familiarity:

Ham. Speak the speech, I pray you, as I pronounced it to you, trippingly on the tongue: but if you mouth it, as many of your players do, I had as lief the town-crier spoke my lines. Nor do not saw the air too much with your hand, thus; but use all gently: for in the very torrent, tempest, and, as I may say, whirlwind of your passion, you must acquire and beget a temperance that may give it smoothness. O, it offends me to the soul to hear a robustious

periwigpated fellow tear a passion to tatters, to very rags, to split the ears
of the groundlings, who, for the most part, are capable of nothing but
inexplicable dumb-shows and noise: I would have such a fellow whipped for
o'er doing Termagant; it out-herods Herod: pray you, avoid it.

First Play. I warrant your honour.

Ham. Be not too tame neither, but let your discretion be your tutor:
suit the action to the word, the word to the action; with this special obser-
vance, that you o'erstep not the modesty of nature: for anything so overdone
is from the purpose of playing, whose end, both at the first and now, was
and is, to hold, as 'twere, the mirror up to nature; to show virtue her own
feature, scorn her own image, and the very age and body of the time his
form and pressure. Now this overdone or come tardy off, though it make
the unskilful laugh, cannot but make the judicious grieve; the censure of
the which one must in your allowance o'erweigh a whole theatre of others.
O, there be players that I have seen play, and heard others praise, and that
highly, not to speak it profanely, that neither having the accent of Christians,
nor the gait of Christian, pagan, nor man, have so strutted and bellowed,
that I have thought some of nature's journeymen had made men, and not
made them well, they imitated humanity so abominably.

First Play. I hope we have reformed that indifferently with us, sir.

Ham. O, reform it altogether. And let those that play your clowns speak
no more than is set down for them: . . .

Hamlet's advice is a plea for quality, and, as such, suggests to
the modern reader the style of acting which he personally has
come to consider best. But examine it carefully, and we
discover that it describes no style of acting. It advocates
moderation and good taste, and could be followed profitably
in every detail by a natural actor, a formal actor, a student of
elocution, a lawyer, a preacher, a member of Congress, or a
coloratura soprano. Through its illustrations, indeed, it suggests
formal more than natural acting because the abuses noted are
more apt to be bred by the former than by the latter. That the
actor should "hold, as 'twere, the mirror up to nature" did not
mean that he should strive to produce naturalistic effects in our
sense of the term: Shakespeare was expressing a *cliché* from
classical criticism, equally applicable to all the arts. Before

yielding to the suggestiveness of Hamlet's advice to the players, one should read the following passage from Heywood's *An Apology for Actors:*

It [play-acting at the Universities] teacheth audacity to the bashfull grammarian, beeing newly admitted into the private colledge, and, after matriculated and entred as a member of the University, and makes him a bold sophister, to argue *pro et contra* to compose his syllogysmes, cathegoricke, or hypotheticke (simple or compound), to reason and frame a sufficient argument to prove his questions, or to defend any *axioma*, to distinguish of any dilemma, and be able to moderate in any argumentation whatsoever.

To come to rhetoricke: it [that is, *acting in the Universities* as before] not onely emboldens a scholler to speake, but instructs him to speake well, and with judgement to observe his commas, colons, and full points; his parentheses, his breathing spaces, and distinctions; to keepe a decorum in his countenance, neither to frowne when he should smile, nor to make unseemely and disguised faces in the delivery of his words; not to stare with his eies, draw awry his mouth, confound his voice in the hollow of his throat, or teare his words hastily betwixt his teeth; neither to buffet his deske like a mad man, nor stand in his place like a livelesse image, demurely plodding, and without any smooth and formal motion. It instructs him to fit his phrases to his action, and his action to his phrase, and his pronuntiation to them both.[8]

Here is all of Hamlet's doctrine, some of it suggested no doubt by Hamlet's own words, but in Heywood's style and Heywood's context how differently it strikes us! To no one could it suggest natural acting. It suggests rather the "bashfull grammarian," later the "bold sophister," docilely imitating his master's paces, faithfully perfecting with *smooth and formal motion* the approved gestures.

All direct contemporary testimony concerning the Elizabethan manner of acting proves, upon analysis, as equivocal as Hamlet's advice to the players. Most of this testimony concerns Tarleton, Kempe, Alleyn, and Burbage. It would be

[8]*An Apology for Actors* (1612). Reprinted for the Shakespeare Society (1841), pp. 28–29.

difficult to base any conclusions upon the comments on Tarleton and Kempe, since they seem to have interested their contemporaries chiefly in their specialized role of clown and gag-man. As to Alleyn and Burbage, their contemporaries were agreed that they were splendid actors. We dare not run with the hare and hunt with the hounds by claiming that the Elizabethans progressed from formal to natural acting, and that Alleyn was of the old formal school and Burbage of the new natural school. Mr. G. B. Harrison has crystallized this body of opinion in his "Shakespeare's Actors,"[9] which makes much of topical and satirical suggestions in Hamlet's advice to the players. But Mr. Harrison's argument is cancelled by Heywood's *Apology* (pp. 29, 43):

And this is the action behoovefull in any that professe this quality, not to use any impudent or forced motion in any part of the body, nor rough or other violent gesture, nor on the contrary to stand like a stiffe starcht man, but to qualify everything according to the nature of the person personated . . . .

Among so many [excellent actors] dead, let me not forget one yet alive, in his time the most worthy famous Maister Edward Allen.

Thus all the inferences respecting Alleyn and Burbage must be reversed, depending upon whether we follow Heywood or Shakespeare. Truly there is not a scintilla of evidence to prove that Alleyn's acting was different in kind or inferior in quality to Burbage's. Both are highly praised, and both in the same general terms. Each is a Proteus for shapes, a Roscius for a voice: little more are we told, of them or their fellows, and that little is not enough. Below I quote the most "specific" matter. Ben Jonson tells us in his famous Epigram that little Sal. Pavy

> . . . did act, what now we moan,
>   Old men so duly
> As, sooth, the Parcae thought him one
>   He play'd so truly.

[9] *Shakespeare and the Theatre.* . . . By Members of the Shakespeare Association (1927), pp. 62–87.

Burbage's elegist affirms:

> Oft haue I seene him, leap into the Graue,
> Suiting the person, which he seem'd to haue
> Of a sadd Louer, with soe true an Eye,
> That theer I would haue sworne, he meant to dye,
> Oft haue I seene him, play this part in ieast,
> Soe liuly, that Spectators, and the rest
> Of his sad Crew, whilst he but seem'd to bleed,
> Amazed, thought even then hee dyed in deed.[10]

Then there is Hamlet again (II, ii, 544–50):

> Is it not monstrous that this player here,
> But in a fiction, in a dream of passion,
> Could force his soul so to his own conceit
> That from her working all his visage wann'd;
> Tears in his eyes, distraction in's aspect,
> A broken voice, and his whole function suiting
> With forms to his conceit?

Forms? What forms? Tears? a broken voice? a "visage wann'd"? the symptoms of emotion, like the inflamed eyes behind the mask of Cicero's actor? For the rest, "his whole function suiting" tells us nothing, nor, in the other passages, does "He play'd so truly," or "Suiting the person, which he seem'd to haue." Nor do Shakespeare's "hold the mirror up to nature" and Heywood's "qualify everything according to the nature of the person personated." We are told *what* the actor did (in the estimation of the spectator), but not *how* he did it. Since the conventions of formal acting will be accepted as just while formal acting prevails, testimony like the above is nugatory.

Equally so is what may be called the German testimony. Fynes Moryson's *Itinerary* with its oft-quoted passages concerning the vogue of English actors across the channel in 1592, and the enthusiastic comments of the foreign spectators them-

---

[10]Edwin Nungezer, *Dictionary of Actors* (1929), p. 74.

selves, have led to such statements as that by Mr. J. Isaacs in his "Shakespeare as Man of the Theatre": "The Germans were impressed by the English naturalistic style of acting and the complete absorption of each actor in his part."[11] Contrasting oddly with this is the comment of one of those supposedly impressed by the "naturalistic style." Wrote Balthasar Paumgartner:

> Here are some English actors whose plays I have seen. They have such splendid good music, and are perfect in their dancing and jumping, whose equal I have never yet seen. There are ten or twelve of them, all richly and magnificently clothed.[12]

We can readily detect how Herr Paumgartner was impressed. There is further comment by the Germans, but none of it proves more than that a nation, laggard in the theatre, was surprised by the professionalism of the English actors and pleased by their showmanship. These actors, speaking a language incomprehensible to their auditors, would increase the element of pantomime in their plays, and the German response has been misinterpreted as a response to naturalistic acting.

Thus far I have referred to the views of three believers in natural Elizabethan acting, but the position of these three is by no means the same. Mr. Granville-Barker makes the appearance of such acting await the appearance of particular qualities in the drama; he denies it to the performers of *Tamburlaine* but grants it to the later performers of *Hamlet*.[13] Mr. Harrison grants it to Burbage but denies it to Burbage's contemporary, Edward Alleyn. But Mr. Isaacs grants it generously even to second-rate English actors performing "pieces and patches"[14] of biblical plays, and moral and romantic interludes, in Germany in 1592. These mutually contradictory positions on the

---

[11]*Shakespeare and the Theatre*, p. 93.   [12]*Ibid.*, p. 92. Quoted by Mr. Isaacs himself.
[13]Tamburlaine, says the critic, is a character "rather to be exhibited than acted," *Prefaces to Shakespeare*, Third Series (1937), *"Hamlet,"* p. 3.
[14]The phrase is Fynes Moryson's.

part of the believers are a commentary upon their grounds of belief.

Actually there is extant not a single piece of analytical description of Elizabethan acting in general, or of an Elizabethan actor in a particular role. Not until we come to Thomas Betterton do we meet criticism by standards, or description that is sophisticated—written by witnesses showing a consciousness of alternatives in style. For a reason that will soon become apparent, a word must be interpolated here concerning Betterton's acting. Betterton was, I believe, the Michel Baron of the English stage. The eighteen-year lapse in regular theatrical performances in England, and the Restoration adaptation of the scenic stage, would have paved the way for innovation, and prevented innovation from being discussed (as in France) as revolutionary. Betterton, though only in his middle twenties and competing with such seasoned pre-Commonwealth actors as Hart and Mohun, was being hailed in 1661 as the "best actor in the world" who does Hamlet and all other parts "beyond imagination."[15] His success alone proves nothing, although it is suggestive. But in the case of Betterton we have, for the first time in England, something more than generalized praise of an actor. We have detailed eye-witness accounts of his acting, and critical commentary, in such works as Steele's *Tatler* (May 2, 1710), Colley Cibber's *Apology*, Antony Aston's "Supplement" to Theophilus Cibber's *Lives of the Actors*, and Davies' *Dramatic Miscellanies*; and from these we can determine that his acting was not only excellent in quality but naturalistic in kind. We are told specifically that he spoke without *tone*,

---

[15]Pepys' Diary, Nov. 4 and Oct. 15. Betterton is said to have been coached in the parts of Hamlet and Henry VIII by Davenant, following respectively methods of Taylor and Lowin (John Downes, *Roscius Anglicanus*, pp. 21, 24), but no more need be inferred than that he received guidance in the reading of lines. Betterton himself sought such guidance when he took over a role formerly played by Hart. See Davies, *Dramatic Miscellanies*, quoted in Anon., *Life and Times of Thomas Betterton* (1888), p. 144.

meaning that he did not entone his lines as did certain Augustan actors whose acting had suffered the relapse from which Garrick was ultimately to rescue it. Betterton's gestures were "few but just." The *just* means little, but the *few* means much, as does a reference to his arms, "which he rarely lifted higher than his stomach." I am quoting Tony Aston rather than the fine appreciation of Steele or the elaborate critique of Cibber, because Aston's attitude is so purely objective. Aston concludes: "Betterton from the time he was dressed, to the end of the play, kept his mind in the same temperament and adaptness as the present character required."[16]

We are now in a position to evaluate the final piece of external evidence for Elizabethan natural acting. It is a passage from Richard Flecknoe's "A Short Discourse of the English Stage," printed with the author's *Love's Kingdom* in 1664. The passage has not been placed by historians in its proper biographical setting, and has done, consequently, considerable mischief. I quote it in such context as it usually provokes:

The German audiences were impressed by the unprecedented naturalism of the acting and the actor's intensity within his part. Richard Flecknoe, at some distance, it is true, gives this description of Richard Burbage who played Lear, Hamlet and Falstaff among other chief parts:

"He was a delightful Proteus, so wholly transforming himself into his part, and putting off himself with his cloathes, as he never (not so much as in the Tyring-house) assum'd himself again until the Play was done. . . .

"He had all the parts of an excellent orator (animating his words with speaking, and speech with action) his Auditors being never more delighted than when he spoke, nor more sorry than when he held his peace; yet even then, he was an excellent Actor still, never falling in his Part when he had done speaking; but with his looks and gesture, maintaining it still unto the heighth."[17]

The phrase "at some distance, it is true," reveals a true desire in the quoter to serve truth, but that he is strongly influenced

[16]Anon., *Thomas Betterton*, pp. 120-122, reprinted from Antony Aston's Supplement to Cibber's *Lives of the Actors*.
[17]J. Isaacs, in *Shakespeare and the Theatre*, p. 113.

by Flecknoe's tribute to Burbage is quite evident. So also have been many others, including Karl Mantzius, who, after observing that Shakespeare would have had "enough influence over the young actor [Burbage] to draw him away from the affected and boisterous manner which was the fashion of the time, and inoculate him with the sound principles which ruled his own writing and acting,"[18] proceeds to quote Flecknoe.

Flecknoe's account of Burbage, I grant, like Aston's of Betterton and Riccoboni's of Baron, postulates natural acting. But what is Flecknoe's testimony worth? We do not know when Flecknoe was born. We know that he lived until 1678. So that even though he was old enough to travel abroad in 1640,[19] or to publish a book in 1626, it remains unlikely that he was more than a boy when Burbage died in 1619. But even assuming that Flecknoe was old enough to form in 1619 (and to retain until 1664) a critical estimate of Burbage's acting, we must still refuse to admit his testimony. Consider the occasion on which he spoke. The portion omitted from the passage as reproduced above runs as follows:

there being as much difference between him and one of our Common Actors, as between a Ballad-singer who onely mouths it, and an excellent singer who knows all his Graces, and can artfully vary and modulate his Voice, even to know how much breath he is to give to every syallable.

The clue lies in the words *one of our Common Actors*, by which Flecknoe, in all probability, meant Thomas Betterton. In 1664 Flecknoe had a grievance against Davenant and Betterton because *Love's Kingdom* had "Expir'd the third Day"[20] and the author had missed his benefit. Now he published the play "not as it was Acted at the Theatre near Lincoln's Inn Field, but as it was written," together with his discourse. Flecknoe's description of *Burbage's* acting is quite as likely a description of

[18] *A History of Theatrical Art*, III (1904), 226–227.
[19] E. K. Chambers, *Elizabethan Stage*, IV, 369.
[20] John Downes, *Roscius Anglicanus*, p. 31.

Betterton's, or of what Betterton was establishing as a standard of acting in 1664. We are certain that Flecknoe knew Betterton's acting, uncertain that he knew Burbage's. Flecknoe was quite capable of employing the most exasperating of all tactics—wounding a man with a weapon from his own armoury.

If the external evidence for natural acting proves tenuous upon examination, so also does the internal evidence—the indications cited in the plays themselves. Consider the following passage from Professor Sprague's *Shakespeare and the Audience*:

Brutus says:

> The angry spot doth glow on Caesar's brow,
> And all the rest look like a chidden train;
> Calphurnia's cheek is pale, and Cicero
> Looks with such ferret and such fiery eyes
> As we have seen him in the Capitol,
> Being cross'd in conference by some senators.
>
> (*Jul.C.*, I. 2. 181)

When one is tempted to think of Elizabethan acting as mere elocution or acrobatics, it might be well to recall those lines.... Hamlet, watching the ghost, speaks of 'how pale he glares,' of his 'piteous action' and of his 'stealing away'; while Gertrude, watching Hamlet, says that his hair 'starts up and stands on end.'[21]

We have here an illustration of the common failure to distinguish between *action* and *acting,* and of the modern tendency to read Elizabethan dramatic lines as if they were stage directions. From Professor Sprague's quotations we may safely conclude that the ghost *steals away,* just as we may conclude from the colloquy at Ophelia's burial that Laertes leaps into the grave, that Hamlet leaps after him, and that Laertes grasps Hamlet by the throat. All this is *action,* and the Elizabethan dramatic line frequently signals for action. But there is a crucial distinction between signalling for action and directing *acting.*

I can imagine a dissertation with the title "Could our Older

[21]Arthur C. Sprague, *Shakespeare and the Audience* (1935), pp. 10-11.

English Actors Turn Pale?" Perhaps such a one exists. Materials are not wanting: we have already noticed how the "visage wann'd" with Hamlet's player, and as late as the eighteenth century Thomas Betterton was accredited with similar virtuosity. A gentleman related to Davies (*Dramatic Miscellanies*) how Betterton's countenance "which was naturally ruddy and sanguine" turned "as pale as his neckcloth" when he played Hamlet confronted by the ghost. Let us compromise the point: sometimes, perhaps, the actors did turn pale, but they could not do so at will. Did an angry spot actually glow on Caesar's brow? Did Calphurnia's cheek turn pale, Caesar's eyes fiery? Did Hamlet's hair actually stand on end? Unless we think so, we must qualify the declarations of the actor speaking, until they lose all significance as indications of what his fellow actors are doing. When Cinna in *Julius Caesar* (II, i, 103–104) says that

> yon grey lines
> that fret the clouds are messengers of day

we do not assume that clouds and grey lines were actually placed on display. No more should we assume that, when the actor representing Brutus spoke, those representing Caesar, Calphurnia, and Cicero displayed respectively a glowing spot, a pale cheek, and a fiery eye—or, indeed, did anything that might withdraw the eyes of the audience from the speaker. To remain inconspicuous seems to be the injunction to the actors in the Prologue to Nashe's *Summer's Last Will and Testament*: ". . . and this I bar, over and besides, that none of you stroke your beards to make action, play with your codpiece points, or stand fumbling on your buttons when you know not how to bestow yourselves." Consider the implications of reading dramatic lines as stage directions. The following is from the *Philoctetes* of Sophocles:

> *Philoctetes*
> Take me, O Earth, a dying man, so near
> His end with sickness that he cannot stand.

Neoptolemus
Methinks in no long time he'll be asleep
For, see, his head sinks backward, and o'er all
His body, look you, trickle beads of sweat,
And from an artery in his wounded foot
The black blood spurts. So let us leave him, friends,
In peace and quiet 'till he fall asleep.[22]

Obviously we must conclude that Greek acting was not elocutionary, and that the Greek actor exercised even greater physiological self-control than did the Elizabethan.

The Elizabethan play is highly descriptive, both of places and of persons. Shakespeare describes a weird night in Rome or a procession of Romans, not the stage of the Globe or the behaviour of a group of actors. There will be "thunder and lightning" on the stage and movement among the players, but not, necessarily, naturalistic effects anywhere. Such stage directions as may be read literally describe acting safely within the formal frame. Characters wring their hands to denote anguish, throw themselves on the ground to denote grief, enter reading a book to denote pensiveness. Queen Katherine in *Henry VIII* (IV, ii) "makes in her sleep signs of rejoicing, and holdeth up her hands to heaven. . . ." We can imagine what her gesture would seem to be if conveyed to us in Shakespeare's blank verse. The descriptive element in the Elizabethan dramatic line, far from being evidence of natural acting, is the exact reverse. It indicates that the speaker, not the speaker's fellow-actors, was charged with the task of implanting an image in the minds of the auditors. We may face the issue squarely by asking ourselves a question. In what modern play, written for actors of the natural school, are there speeches resembling that of Brutus? Would not such speeches seem absurdly redundant? The modern playwright, to an extent not dreamed of by the Elizabethans, shares his task with his actors and guides them, when necessary, by his stage directions.

My purpose now is to sketch the case for formal acting. I

[22]*Sophocles*, trans. F. Storr, 2 vols. (1924), II, 433–435.

offer it as a target to those whose case for natural acting I have been using as a target. My first piece of evidence is documentary and, I believe, "new." As preface to a play still in manuscript, *The Cyprian Conqueror, or The Faithless Relict*, there exists a brief discussion of the art of acting. After cataloguing the various voices to be employed on the stage, the anonymous author proceeds to gesture:

The other parts of action is in ye gesture, wch must be various, as required; as in a sorrowfull parte, ye head must hang downe; in a proud, ye head must bee lofty; in an amorous, closed eies, hanging downe lookes, & crossed armes, in a hastie, fumeing, & scratching ye head &c. . . . [23]

There is no proof that the author was familiar with the popular stage, although his attack on "ye phanatick gang of histriomastiques," his resentment that "ye pretended illuminist, or severe nonconformist carpe at playes," suggest that he was, at least as a patron, and that he wrote after, but not long after, Prynne's attack of 1633.

Here, then, we have the earliest specific instructions for acting extant in English, and the writer's conception is of formal, not natural, acting. I am retarded, however, from experiencing that sensation of joy which comes to the student when he has unearthed an authentic scrap of paper. Provoked by my manuscript into investigating later manuals of acting, I have been disturbed to discover that they *continue* to teach formal acting. Charles Gildon considered his *Life of Thomas Betterton* (1710) the first such manual in English, and he actually fathered upon Betterton instructions like the following (p. 43): "A lifting or tossing of the Head is the Gesture of Pride and Arrogance. Carrying the Head aloft is the sign of Joy, Victory, and Triumph . . ." etc. Scarcely noticeable in the book because of its casual inclusion (p. 41) is the significant remark of Mrs. Bradshaw, to a friend of the author, that "she endeavour'd first to make her self Mistress of her Part, and left the Figure

[23]British Museum, Sloane MS 3709.

and Action to Nature." Curll's *History of the English Stage* (1741), the whole work, in this instance, fathered upon Betterton, simply repeats Gildon. In 1807, Henry Siddons, the not-so-famous son of a famous mother, translated *Illustrations of Rhetorical Gesture and Action* from the German of M. Engel. The cuts reveal a series of attitudes best calculated to express the emotions, and although sponsored by an actor in the great age of Kemble, they picture acting formalized beyond belief. *Joy* is portrayed by a young lady in an Empire dress who seems to have been arrested midway in one of Miss Bradbrook's "capers." In 1882, Gustave Garcia, Professor of Singing and Declamation at the Royal Academy of Music, published his *The Actor's Art* and actually dedicated the book to Henry Irving. The cuts are somewhat better in draughtsmanship, but the book is no different in kind from that of Siddons. Mr. Garcia tells us that, "Anger as it becomes more violent and turns into a passion, will assume a different expression and from Attitude Fig. 38 will pass to that of Figs. 40 and 41." Garcia's attitude for *Listening* (Fig. 64) is almost identical with Siddons' attitude for *Expectation*. The natural basis of the attitude is evidently the tendency of a human being to crane forward and cup his hand to his ear. Eschewing vulgarity by removing the hand a foot from the ear, disposing the arm not thus in use by extending it out and downward in a graceful curve, and placing the feet in the first movement of a waltz step, the attitude reveals the tendency of attitudes in general. The same one is illustrated once more, this time under the caption *Listening to a Bird*, in what must be the apotheosis of all such manuals of acting: Edmund Shaftesbury's *Lessons in the Art of Acting* (Washington, D.C., 1889). Shaftesbury begins with some sensible remarks on the limitations of the Delsarte system of dramatic attitudes, and makes a good distinction between "Objective" (formal) gesture, suitable for elocutionists, and "Subjective" (natural) gesture, suitable, but only to the limit of 50 per cent of the total gestures, says he, for regular actors.

But as his book continues, the author seems to forget entirely
about subjective gesture. Chapter XLIV deals with the twelve
kneeling attitudes, XLV with the twelve sitting attitudes,
XLVIII with the seven intellectual (!) attitudes, XXVII with the
seven methods of falling to the floor. The cuts are delectable,
especially *Goodbye* (32nd attitude), *Reverie* (102nd attitude),
and *Frenzy* (90th attitude): "This attitude is made by inclining
the head backward, looking up; and clutching the hair with
both hands." I have not traced any later works of the type, but
I am certain that similar ones exist at the present day, for circu-
lation in the rural areas.

If manuals like those described were to be taken at face value
as indicating how actors used to act, our task would be to prove,
not that formal acting once graced the English stage, but that
it had ever ceased to do so. What these books really prove is
that, although acting may cease to be formal, teachers of acting
will never cease trying to formalize it; and my Preface to
The Cyprian Conqueror is a reminder.

In Elizabethan times, to an extent never afterwards equalled,
acting was taught. "I graunt your action, though it be a kind of
mechanical labour, yet wel done tis worthy of praise . . . ,"
said Robert Greene in 1590;[24] and more than two decades later
Thomas Heywood, an actor, still thought of acting as "a kind
of mechanical labour." Actors, said he,

. . . should be rather schollers, that, though they cannot speake well, know
how to speake, or else to have that volubility that they can speake well,
though they understand not what, and so both imperfections may by instruction be helped and amended. . . .

Heywood even believed in the efficacy of acting manuals:

Labericus [i.e. Laberius Decimus?] was an excellent poet and rare actor,
who writ a book of the gesture and action to be used by the tragedians and
comedians in performance of every part in his native humor.[25]

[24]*Francescos Fortunes* . . . (1590), p. 132.
[25]*Apology for Actors*, pp. 42, 43.

At a vital formative period in English theatrical history, school-masters exercised considerable influence. Plays were performed by boys for "learning and utterance sake"[26] and, incidentally, for court amusement. No doubt, actors as well as authors were "first instructed in the University, after drawne like a novice to these abuses."[27] What kind of influence upon the creation of an English school of acting would have been exerted by such "dramatic coaches" as Udall, Edwards, Hunnis, Westcote, and Lyly? The answer is suggested by part of Edwards' Prologue to his Chapel play *Damon and Pithias* (1571):

> So correspondent to their kind their speeches ought to be,
> Which speeches well-pronounced, with action lively framed—
> If this offend the looker on, let Horace then be blamed,
> Which hath our author taught at school, from whom he doth not swerve,
> In all such kind of exercise decorum to observe.

It is next to certain that Edwards and his kind would have sought classical authority.

Among the manuals of acting previously discussed, the earlier ones seem to have a common source. Gildon mentions "a learned Jesuit who wrote on this subject," whom I suspect to be M. Hedelin, Abbot of Aubignic, although no catalogue of gestures appears in the only work of Hedelin available to me.[28] More important, Gildon mentions as the authority of the learn-ed Jesuit the Roman teacher Quintilian. Quintilian and Cicero are both utilized by the author of the Preface to *The Cyprian Conqueror*. The latter takes his catalogue of voices from Julius Pollux's *Onomasticon*, a Greek compendium of the second century. Everywhere, in Heywood as in the earlier contro-versialists on the stage, is there a seeking for authority in the ancients: Roscius, Æsopus, and Cicero are names constantly invoked.

[26]John Northbrooke, *Treatise* ... (1577), p. 103.
[27]Stephen Gosson, *School of Abuse* (1579), p. 19.
[28]*The Whole Art of the Stage*, Eng. trans. (1684).

The classics provided no manual of acting, but they did provide manuals of oratory, in Cicero's *De Oratore* and Quintilian's *Institutio Oratoria*. These must have exerted a large influence. Both Cicero and Quintilian are equivocal upon the relationship of acting and oratory. The orator, says Cicero at one point, avoids "the gesture of the stage," but at another, he says "the gesture almost of the best actors, is required," and at another, "Who can deny that the gesture and grace of Roscius are necessary in the orator's action and deportment?"[29] Quintilian faithfully duplicates his idol's inconsistencies. "For what can be less becoming to an orator than modulations that recall the stage . . .?" he asks, but then he teaches that aversion is to be expressed "by turning away the head and by thrusting out our hands as though to repel the thought. . . ."[30] The schoolmasters would have found no clear-cut distinction between oratory and acting in their authorities, and the discussion of the gestures of oratory would have seemed apposite to their needs. Had not Roscius himself, according to Valerius Maximus, learned his craft in the forum by observing the oratorical exhibitions?[31] A passage like the following from Quintilian would have been eagerly attended by a Richard Edwards:

. . . Roscius was rapid and Aesopus weighty in his delivery, because the former was a comic and the latter a tragic actor. The same rule applies to the movements. Consequently on the stage young men and old, soldiers and married women all walk sedately, while slaves, maid-servants, parasites and fishermen are more lively in their movements.[32]

Here is a *rule*, and teachers love rules. It is significant that throughout the Elizabethan period, the same word *action* is used alike to designate acting and oratorical gesture. Edward Alleyn's gratulatory speech to James I on his entry into London

[29]*De Oratore* (Bohn's Classical Library, pp. 175, 215, 398).
[30]*Institutio Oratoria* (Loeb Classics, IV, 1922, 275, 283).
[31]G. K. G. Henry, "Roman Actors," *SP*, XVI (1919), 351.
[32]*Institutio Oratoria* (Loeb Classics, IV, 303).

was delivered "with excellent action and a well-tuned, audible voice."[33] Even the words *actor* and *orator* tended to coalesce. In Overbury's (i.e., John Webster's?) "An Excellent Actor" (1615) we are told, probably of Burbage, that "Whatsoever is commendable in the Grave Orator, is most exquisitely perfect in him; for by a full and significant action of body, he charmes our attention."[34]

Testimony that seems principally to bear upon the style of acting among boys might seem far-fetched were it not probable that men and boys both acted alike. The influence of the schools and classical authority might be disregarded except for an extremely important piece of related evidence—*the continued success of the child actors*. At the very moment that *Hamlet* was first performed, Burbage and his fellows were being seriously rivalled by companies consisting entirely of young boys. These boys, though they performed comedies mainly, performed tragedies as well: *Antonio's Revenge, Cupid's Revenge, Byron's Conspiracy, Bussy D'Ambois, Sophonisba, The Insatiate Countess,* and *Philotas,* to mention the plays extant. That boys were considered capable of performing tragic roles even side by side with adult actors is evidenced by Cleopatra, Desdemona, the Duchess of Malfi, and numerous other important feminine characters in Elizabethan tragedies. Common sense dictates that Elizabethan boys were no different essentially from boys today—who can act well when cast as children, but who *cannot* succeed in the "imaginative interpretation" of adult roles. Yet Elizabethan boys, in adult roles, successfully competed with or co-operated with adult actors. Here is an anomaly. I quote Professor Hillebrand's explanation of the anomaly:

The drama had made tremendous strides toward maturity and complexity; the art of acting had been enriched by the labors of Tarleton, Alleyn, and Burbage; the public was becoming rapidly trained to the fine points of dramaturgy and acting, and was inevitably bound toward finer sophistica-

[33]Thomas Dekker, *Magnificent Entertainment* (1604).
[34]Ed. E. K. Chambers, *Elizabethan Stage*, IV, 257-258.

tion, aided by the great decade which had opened. London in 1600 was a far different place from what it was in 1585, even in 1590. How could people now feel toward child actors as they had felt before? Even admitting that the Jacobean spectators were as satisfied of the fitness of boys to play women as the Elizabethans had been, surely they found no illusion when boys impersonated men, they who knew Burbage and Alleyn. Boys on the stage must have seemed to them largely what boys on the stage now seem to us— masqueraders. . . . I cannot help feeling that the fundamental attraction of the boy actors for the Jacobean public was the whimsical charm of a masquerade. . . . [To tolerate boys now] . . . we would have to put ourselves in the frame of mind of Italian laborers at a marionette show, lose our sense of unreality in a deep interest in the play, and forget that the puppets are not the heroes they pretend to be.[35]

Observable in the passage is the fact that one supposition— that the appeal of the boy actors was merely "whimsical charm"—has been forced upon the author by another supposition—that the audience who knew Burbage and Alleyn "was becoming rapidly trained to the fine points of dramaturgy and acting." "Whimsical charm" fails to satisfy me as an explanation of a vogue that endured so long and was ended principally by the difficulty of keeping talented boys from growing up—and which leaves *unexplained* the success of the boys in the adult companies. My explanation of the apparent adequacy of the Elizabethan boy actor is simply *formal acting*. In formal acting, as distinct from natural acting ("imaginative interpretation"), boys could successfully compete. If puppets they were, then in 1600 those at the Blackfriars were simply somewhat smaller than those at the Globe.

One hint of the probability of formal acting may be disposed of briefly. This is the existence and persistence of dumbshow in the plays, indicating a tendency among playwrights to segregate in their minds two methods of conveying intelligence: by pantomime and by dialogue. Dumbshows display no tendency to disappear from plays in the period supposed to mark increased

[35]Harold N. Hillebrand, "The Child Actors," *University of Illinois Studies in Language and Literature*, XI (1926), no. 1, 271, 274.

naturalness in acting; and whereas the earlier dumbshows were symbolical, the later ones were used "to present events necessary to the plot, but not easily included in dialogue form."[36] There is something suggestive in the dumbshow, in the actor's ceasing to speak while he concentrates on *acting*.

Finally, and perhaps most important, though the argument need not be elaborated, the open-air theatre of Shakespeare's day, with its unlocalized, relatively unadorned, and centrally placed stage, was better suited to formal than to natural acting. That the boy companies acted formally I consider almost a prima facie case, yet until nearly the end of Shakespeare's active career the boys monopolized the indoor theatres. The position of Burbage was more nearly that of his ancient fellow in the Greek amphitheatre than of his modern fellow behind a proscenium arch. He was almost surrounded by his audience. He was part of a statuary group. His attitudes must have been statuesque, and his gestures such as would convey meaning to the considerable portion of his audience who could not see his face. The whimsical smile, the arched brow, the significant sidelong glance would not do. He had to act with his body. We sometimes assume that, in the open-air theatres, seeing would be easy, hearing difficult, but the opposite may be the truth. The adult actors were occasionally marked as "tearthroats," but one[37] who understands acoustics has told me that, with the balconies occupied, the acoustics of the Globe should have been the well-nigh perfect acoustics of a soft-surfaced well. But a well is not to be recommended for visibility, especially on wintry London afternoons. The playhouses of the Restoration were relatively small and well-lighted, and Thomas Betterton could afford to keep his hands below his waist-line. The modern actor in the glare of footlights can afford to reduce

---

[36]F. A. Foster, "Dumb Show in Elizabethan Drama before 1620," *Englische Studien*, XLIV (1912), 16.
[37]My former colleague Professor John Dolman.

his gesture almost to the natural movements of a visitor to our drawing room.

The opinion is almost universal that acting made great strides during the last decade of the sixteenth century. I share that belief, although I believe we should be cautious in defining the nature of these strides. The arts, in general, do not develop on strictly parallel lines—as the illustrations in volumes of Elizabethan poetry should serve to prove. Let us suppose that a reader of *The Shepheardes Calender,* appreciative of poetical art, was aware that the original edition was illustrated, but had not seen those, or any other Elizabethan illustrations. What pictures of delicate tracery would he imagine—until he saw the illustrations. Most of us incline to deprecate the Droeshout engraving of Shakespeare (we who have not seen Shakespeare), while Heming, Condell, Jonson, and the rest (who had seen Shakespeare) seemed reasonably content with the engraving. In the end, the appreciative reader of *The Shepheardes Calender* will approve the modern printer's tendency to reproduce the original illustrations rather than to set his own art department to work: the originals have their own appropriateness. Creizenach has said:"... it is obvious that when the old pieces written in doggerel like *Cambyses* or *Appius and Virginia* were replaced by the tragedies of Marlowe, Kyd, and the youthful Shakespeare, a complete revolution must have taken place in acting as well as play-writing."[38] But why a complete revolution? Why, at any rate, a change from formal to natural acting? Why not simply an improvement in formal acting—an increase in grace, in restraint, in mastery of the stylized gesture, and, above all, in the clear, musical, and expressive reading of lines?

The imaginative description of Elizabethan acting most satisfying to me, from a purely aesthetic viewpoint, is one by the late Professor Thorndike,[39] and it is a description of formal

[38]W. Creizenach, *The English Drama in the Age of Shakespeare* (1916), p. 395.
[39]Ashley H. Thorndike, *Shakespeare's Theatre* (1916), pp. 402-403.

acting. Formal acting is not bad in itself. It only seems bad when it represents, as it must needs in modern times, the resort of a third-rate actor or teacher of acting, or a disharmonious intrusion upon an established contemporary ideal. Burbage, I believe, read Shakespeare's lines better than any actor has done since. The basis of my belief, so far as it has a basis other than a pious wish, is not that Burbage had Shakespeare for his coach, but that formal acting would have released him from the fancied necessity of making the lines sound like natural speech (which they are *not*) and of accompanying them with natural gestures (upon which much of an actor's efforts and an audience's attention are now dissipated). If we think of formal acting truly skilful, and an Elizabethan audience completely in accord with it, we find that we have nothing to pity—indeed, perhaps something to envy.

DATE DUE